LITTLE LEAGUE®
DRILLS AND
STRATEGIES

IMAGINATIVE PRACTICE DRILLS
to Improve Skills and Attitiude

NED McINTOSH and RICH CROPPER

Contemporary Books

Chicago   New York   San Francisco   Lisbon   London   Madrid   Mexico City
Milan   New Delhi   San Juan   Seoul   Singapore   Sydney   Toronto

Library of Congress Cataloging-in-Publication Data

McIntosh, Ned.
      Little League drills and strategies / Ned McIntosh and Rich Cropper.—Rev. ed.
            p.   cm. — (Little League baseball guides)
      Includes index.
      ISBN 0-07-141077-5
         1. Little League Baseball   2. Baseball for children—Coaching—United
States.   3. Baseball for children—Training—United States.   I. Cropper, Rich.
II. Title.   III. Series.

      GV880.5 .M338   2002
      796.357'62—dc21   2002035104

All interior photographs by David Orbock, Village Gallery, Towson, Maryland, unless otherwise noted

      2 3 4 5 6 7 8 9 0   AGM/AGM   2 1 0 9 8 7 6 5 4

ISBN 0-07-141077-5

McGraw-Hill books are available at special quantity discounts to use as premiums and sales promotions, or for use in corporate training programs. For more information, please write to the Director of Special Sales, Professional Publishing, McGraw-Hill, Two Penn Plaza, New York, NY 10121-2298. Or contact your local bookstore.

This book is printed on acid-free paper.

To the boys and girls of
The Berlin, Maryland, Little League

And especially to our favorite Berlin players,
who represent all four divisions of that league:
Parker and Duncan McIntosh and
Anna and Richie Cropper

Pride of Berlin Little League: (from left) Parker, Ned, and Duncan McIntosh; and Anna, Rich, and Richie Cropper

Contents

Introduction

This is a revised edition of one of three books on Little League Baseball that I wrote between 1986 and 1993. *Managing Little League Baseball* was revised in 2000; an updated edition of *The Little League Guide to Tee Ball* is also scheduled for release in 2003. For this second edition of *Little League Drills and Strategies*, I've added a coauthor, Rich Cropper, and changed the venue to Berlin, Maryland, where I've lived since my retirement and where two of my grandsons, Parker and Duncan, play Little League ball. I volunteered to be a coach in Berlin Little League and now assist the manager of their team. Rich is a veteran coach in Berlin Little League, having coached his son Richie through Tee Ball, Rookie League, Minor League, and Major League. He also has a daughter, Anna, who is starting her Little League career in Tee Ball. Between us, Rich and I have a combined thirty years of Little League managing experience spanning two generations.

Many changes have occurred in Little League since I started coaching in the 1980s. When I was coaching the first of my three sons, there was no Tee Ball, and nine was the minimum age for boys and girls to play Little League baseball. Players from ages nine through twelve all played on the same team. The smallest nine-year-

It starts with Tee Ball, where anything can happen and usually does.

old was often intimidated by the biggest twelve-year-old and played only the mandatory two innings in the field and one turn at bat.

Farsighted directors in Little League saw the wisdom of helping youngsters to learn fundamentals and also have fun, and so they adjusted the structure to accommodate different skill levels that allowed them to compete more comfortably. The program starts with Tee Ball at age five, where every player on the squad gets to bat in succession. They hit off the tee, which means that the ball is put in play in nearly every at-bat. Fielders have to make defensive plays, baserunners circle the bases, and lots of whooping and hollering occurs, both on the field and in the stands. It is exciting, everyone has fun, and the score is inconsequential.

Then the players advance to the so-called Rookie League, normally at the age of seven and eight, and learn to hit pitched balls from a pitching machine or thrown by a coach. The next level of play is called the Minor League, normally for players aged nine and ten, where there is competitive action mixed with developmental instruction. And finally there is the Major League, normally for players aged eleven and twelve, who compete at the highest skill level, with the World Series of Little League their ultimate dream.

With respect to defining ages at each skill level, we say "normally" because there are exceptions in cases where chronological age differs from coordination age. For example, a gifted athlete of ten could play in the Major League, while an eleven-year-old whose coordination has not caught up with his growth could benefit from another year in the Minor League. It makes sense to let kids play where their skill level fits best.

We appreciate the contributions of several others who are active in youth baseball in other parts of the country. From St. Matthews,

This is Berlin Little League baseball, played the same way three million kids play it in more than 100 countries throughout the world.

Kentucky, Mike Powers has provided some data, based on his many years of Little League coaching experience, especially in his summer instructional league. From Santa Rosa, California, Johnpaul McIntosh-King, former professional baseball pitcher (and my son-in-law), has contributed, in the chapter on pitching, his know-how on teaching the pitching of breaking balls without straining a young pitcher's arm.

We are grateful to "Woody" Bunting, longtime president of the Berlin Little League, and his cooperative board of directors, managers, coaches, and umpires for allowing us to use their league—in its seventeenth year—as the model for this book. In this book the Berlin Little Leaguers will be the stars, appearing in all of the action shots. Not every organization in the international family of Little Leagues does it the same. But the Berlin Little League does it well and enthusiastically embraces the coaching philosophy to which this book is dedicated: "Keep it simple, and make it fun."

—Ned McIntosh

LITTLE LEAGUE® DRILLS AND STRATEGIES

STRATEGY FOR PRESEASON PLANNING

A parent/manager needs to do a great deal of planning *before* the season begins. The first official event of the Berlin Little League, and most other leagues, is registration, normally held in the month of February. Then tryouts are held in early March, followed shortly thereafter by the player drafts. A savvy manager does some preseason homework and gets involved in every preseason activity of the league.

Registration

Registration, tryouts, and player draft are familiar terms in the sporting world that are utilized in every sport at every level. And the same kind of "homework" is required in preparation for each. A local league should market the unique opportunity of participation in Little League through publicity to reach the maximum number of children. Good relations with the local media, schools, and community organizations is essential. It requires the combined efforts of the members of the local Little League board of directors to make sure that the word is spread and enthusiasm generated that will stimulate local youngsters to want to participate.

We recommend that the schools be asked to cooperate by distributing flyers, printed by the league, to all league-age children to take home to their parents. That is one way to be assured that the parents of all eligible children receive the necessary information about the Little League opportunity. Some leagues provide registration forms to be distributed via the children to their parents, with the instructions that the parent should bring the completed form, along with their child's birth certificate, at the designated time and place. Alternate registration dates should be offered. The Berlin Little League, with the cooperation of the City of Berlin, has registration for four consecutive Saturday mornings in February at City Hall. The advantage of spreading out the registration period is that every interested child has a chance to sign up. It also allows the league officials more one-on-one time with parents to explain what they should expect. This is particularly important for first-time Little League parents. At the Berlin Little League registration, the parents are reminded that all managers, coaches, and league officials are volunteers, and that parents will also be expected to participate in one or more of the various volunteer opportunities—from coaching to taking a turn at the refreshment stand.

They are also informed that the players and parents are expected to participate in the fund-raising programs of the league. Since the registration fee does not begin to cover the total cost for a child's participation, most of the funding for the league comes from volunteer sponsors, such as local businesses and community organizations. Fund-raising, however, continues to play an important part. At the Berlin Little League registration, boxes of candy bars are provided, and players are expected to sell their quota. Raffle tickets are also sold to the parents, then sold at all community events. Berlin Little League includes 25 teams: six Major League, seven

Minor League, six Rookie League, and six Tee Ball teams. It also supports three Junior League and one Senior League team. The Berlin Little League complex includes four Little League–size fields, one of which is lighted; two Tee Ball fields; a Junior/Senior–size lighted field; three batting cages; a refreshment stand; and an equipment building. Portable toilets are set up at strategic locations throughout the complex. It provides recreation for more than 430 boys and girls, and its annual budget exceeds $38,000. A lot of fund-raising and sponsorship is needed to run such a large organization.

Managers should volunteer to help at registration. It gives them the first opportunity to meet new players and their parents. Conversations with both parent and child can provide the manager with information that will be helpful in evaluating a new player's potential. It is also a great recruiting opportunity for finding volunteer coaches to help. In the experience of both coauthors, one manager, two parent/coaches, and a team mother are a desirable combination to handle all of the details of managing a team.

Scouting Talent

The manager who waits for tryouts to evaluate potential team members could be disappointed in several ways. Frequently, particularly in northern climates, tryouts are held on cold days, when the players are dressed for winter and are not able to show off their skills for a spring/summer sport. Tryouts that are brought indoors to a school gymnasium are only marginally successful.

The smart manager will have started making his scouting notes a year in advance. A Major League manager will have watched some Minor League games in the previous season and talked with the Minor League managers about their best players. If there is a Minor League tournament ending the season, the manager should make a point of scouting for next year's team by watching the best players showcase their talents. A parent/manager who is new to the area, and/or new to Little League, will be at a disadvantage in not having had the opportunity to do scouting during the preceding season. However, there is nothing to prevent a new manager from calling the team managers from the previous year and asking their advice on drafting youngsters who played for them and will be in this year's draft. The new manager will still be able to scout, along with the experienced managers, at other local youth sports competition—for example, soccer, football, and basketball games. Even though each sport has its own skills, the physically well-coordinated youngster will stand out in every sport. Any coach of a youth sport acknowledges that physical coordination comes to different children at different ages. Being able to spot the kids who have good eye, arm, leg, and body coordination for their age level is a scouting talent managers should cultivate. And the smart manager will not be bashful about talking to coaches of other youth sports and asking for evaluations of kids they have coached who will be signing up for Little League in the spring.

In addition to being on the lookout for kids who are *generally* well coordinated, the manager is well advised to look *specifically* for potentially good pitchers. It is generally conceded by baseball aficionados, at every level of the game, that pitching contributes more than 50 percent to a winning team's success. Consequently, a manager should make a note of any big, strong, well-coordinated youngster. Pitchers in action cannot be observed in the Rookie or Tee Ball Leagues, since player-pitching is not utilized in either. However, the infielder who can make a strong, accurate throw to first base is worth noting. Good pitchers first show their stuff in Minor League play. Normally they are among the bigger players who can use size and weight to good advantage in throwing a hard fastball.

If there are any instructional baseball summer camps in your area, contact the coaches who run them and ask for their recommendations on kids they coached who will be eligible for your draft. Normally the better ballplayers will be attracted to these camps.

Tryouts

Tryouts are normally arranged to allow managers to see each prospect perform five skills: hitting, fielding a grounder, throwing the ball to first base, catching the ball at first base, and catching fly balls. In the Berlin tryouts, two pitching machines are used in tryouts—one for hitting and the other, tilted upward, to toss up fly balls. The machines are set to deliver the ball at the same speed to each player. In the drill of fielding grounders and throwing to first,

At tryouts, a "rookie" hits, while coaches with clipboards take notes.

a coach hits a grounder, and the player fields it and throws it to first. Players stand in line and wait for their turns to be the fielder and the first baseman, respectively. The players wear numbers, which are pinned to their jerseys when they register at the tryout, and the number of the participating player in each drill is called out, so the managers can score each player as they perform. To prepare for the player draft, the managers then add this data to what information they may have already documented in their "scouting reports" on each player.

It should be noted that the precise way in which registration, tryouts, and the draft of players are conducted may vary from league to league. Recommendations are made to presidents of each league in the *Operating Manual*, provided by Little League Baseball, Inc., but a local league has some freedom to adopt local rules. New managers need to find out how these important functions are performed in their local league.

Preseason Practice

As soon as the draft is completed and you have the names and phone numbers of your players, we recommend that you hold a meeting of your players and their parents. This gives you an opportunity to explain the philosophy of "Keep it simple, make it fun" and to recruit parents to help, if you have not already lined up your staff. In the final chapter of this book, we outline how to guarantee a winning season for the team; it revolves around a plan of practice, practice, and more practice. Obviously, that requires cooperative dedication on the part of your parents to get their children to and from practice. Where there are transportation problems, you can ask their cooperation in working out car pools. In our experience, the children do not object to frequent practices, particularly if you make them fun. The only potential problem is transportation, which hopefully you and the parents can work out. You can remind them that if their children are picked for the All-Star team at the end of the season, they will be asked to attend daily practice sessions; and if they play competitive sports in school, daily practice is expected. There is actually more reason, when children are at the developmental age for learning baseball, to have frequent practices to learn the basic skills they will be using throughout the baseball season and beyond.

Scheduling practice time on a field may create a problem, depending on the number of fields and teams, but a little ingenuity can help. If you schedule a batting practice, the batting cages can be used, instead of a field, and the times for players to bat can be staggered. You can also have one coach supervising players hitting into a fence, as they wait their turn in the batting cage. If you schedule a practice for catching fly balls, all you need is a level field. School fields and soccer fields are another option. If you schedule a "skull session," as discussed in Chapter 8, either your home or a room in a school or community building can be used. If the commitment to practice, practice, practice is there on the part of players, parents, and coaches, it can be scheduled on a daily basis until the season starts. Particularly with the skills that automatically improve with repetition, such as batting and catching fly balls, your team will have a decided advantage over the others if you have practiced every day. And that advantage will continue and increase, after the season begins, if you continue to schedule daily practices on the days on which games are not scheduled. Do you know any professional or school team that doesn't practice every day?

All teams parade down Main Street, accompanied by fire trucks and police cars, as "Hometown Heroes" are honored.

Opening Day

Little League opening day has become a rite of spring in thousands of cities across the country. It begins with a parade in which all teams, in their bright new uniforms, march through town. A manager and staff can use the opportunity to begin to instill competitive team spirit by designing creative team banners to display during the parade.

In 2002, Little League, Inc., encouraged all leagues to add a patriotic theme to their opening day parade, and in recognition of the events of September 11, 2001, dedicate their parades to their "Hometown Heroes"—the police, firemen and rescue squads of their communities. In the Berlin, Maryland, parade, the fire trucks, police cars, and rescue vans drove in the parade, and symbolically the local New York Yankees team led the parade, each player waving an American flag. The parade ended at the ball field complex, where a tent had been set up for the opening day ceremony. The traditional singing of the national anthem was followed by the assembled players reciting the Little League Pledge. Brief remarks followed, including the presentation of recognition plaques to the heads of the local police, fire, and rescue squads. Then it was "play ball" for the rest of the day, as the season officially opened in all divisions.

Preseason "Skull" Training

The importance of mentally understanding the game cannot be stressed enough. Kids who become fans of the game, as well as participants, will enjoy it more, in both roles, if they are taught the rules and the game strategies that make the game so interesting.

Following the philosophy of "making it fun," skull sessions with your players can be made fun with games and quizzes. We recommend you start holding skull sessions as early as possible. If your league allows age-eligible players to be retained by the same team they played for during the previous season, then a continuing manager of that team can start holding skull sessions with those players—who will be the nucleus of this year's team—while there is still snow on the ground. Getting them back into the game of baseball *mentally*, after a year of playing other sports, will return dividends as they ease back into the game *physically*. Then, when you have your first skull session after the draft, with the addition of your new players, the returning players will recognize their importance as role models to their new teammates.

At the end of each of four chapters in *Managing Little League Baseball* there are quizzes. The chapters are about rules, hitting, baserunning, and defense. An inexpensive prize—like a baseball, batting gloves, or baseball cards—can provide an incentive to encourage players to score best in the quiz, while the consensus results of each quiz can show a manager what skills need to be emphasized at outdoor practice. A baseball diamond, drawn on a large sheet of paper, can serve as a game board, and red and black checker pieces used to represent defensive players and offensive runners. At the end of each skull session, you can create game situations on the board and then ask players to explain what should happen, defensively and offensively. For example: With one out and runners on second and third, the batter hits a fly ball to left.

- What does each of the runners do?
- Where does the outfielder throw the ball?
- Who backs up the catcher on the throw to him?

Just as practice, practice, and more practice helps players learn the *physical* baseball skills, repetition, repetition, and more repetition, teaches them the basic *mental* skills of the game.

The Rules

The official *Little League Rule Book* is 82 pages, and that doesn't even include the special rules for tournament play. Obviously, kids can't be expected to know and understand all the rules, but there are a few they should understand because they will encounter them frequently in game situations. There are 15 rules we recommend you cover in a skull session on the rules:

- Mandatory Playing Rule (Regulation IV [i] and Rule 3.03)
- Pitching Restrictions (Regulation VI)
- Behavior Toward Umpires and Other Team (Rules 4.06 through 4.08)
- Use of Protective Equipment (Rules 1.16 and 1.17)

- Location of the Strike Zone (Rule 2.0—definitions)
- Batter's Proper Position in the Batter's Box (Rule 6.03 and definitions)
- Batter or Runner Is Out when Hit by a Batted Ball before a Fielder Touches It (Rule 6.05 [f] and 7.08 [f])
- Runner Interference (Rule 7.08 [b])
- Fielder Obstruction (Rule 2.0—definitions; Rule 7.06 [a], [b])
- When Two Runners Occupy Same Base (Rule 7.03)
- Tagging Up on a Fair or Foul Ball Caught (Rule 7.08 [d])
- Force Play and Removal of Force (Rule 7.08 [e])
- Infield Fly Rule (Rule 2.0—definitions)
- Overrunning First Base (Rule 7.08 [c])
- Runner Leaving Base Too Soon (Rule 7.13)

If the technical language of the rule book is difficult to convey to youngsters, we recommend you refer to Chapter 3 of *Managing Little League Baseball*, where the rationale and some examples of each of these rule are explained.

Hitting

There are a few rules about hitting that are known and understood by experienced baseball players but need to be taught, with repetition, to new players:

- It is bat speed, not weight, that makes a good hitter, so pick a light bat you can swing fast.
- With the count three balls and no strikes, take (don't swing at) the next pitch.
- With the count two strikes and no balls, choke up on the bat and concentrate on making contact with the next ball in the strike zone.
- Keep your eye on the ball. Follow it from the pitcher's release.

- Believe that you will hit the ball, and you will—if not this time at bat, then the next time.

Baserunning

How many times have you heard the following advice? You may tell it to your new players for the first time in a skull session, and have to keep reminding them (and the experienced ones) when they are on base:

- When there are two outs, run on anything.
- When there are no outs (or one out), and you are forced, run on a ground ball and and hold up on a fly.
- When in doubt whether to slide, slide.
- When you get a walk, run to first and take a turn.

Defense

Here are some old coaching tips that will probably be new to rookies when you pass them on in a skull session:

- Play the ball—don't let it play you.
- Look the ball into your glove.
- Cover the ball in your glove with your bare hand.
- On every hit ball, cover the ball or a base.
- If you're not covering the ball, back up your teammate who is.
- If you can't catch the ball, block it and keep it in front of you.
- Throw to two bases ahead of the lead runner when you field a hit from the outfield.
- With runners on base, always try to get the lead runner out.

Make your skull sessions interactive, not like school. Keep them simple and make them fun. Invite your players to suggest situations, perhaps from their own experience in games, that illustrate a point you are making. Keep skull sessions a part of your coaching throughout the season, not just in the preseason. Game situations will occur that will reinforce the points you make in your skull sessions. A rained-out game or practice is the perfect time to hold an impromptu skull session during the season.

If you thought your duties as a manager started at the first outdoor team practice, the foregoing discussion should convince you that there are many things you could and should do, preseason, that can help you and your team have a more enjoyable, more successful season.

13

A Little League player throws out the first pitch at Berlin Little League Night at the local professional baseball stadium.

2

DRILLS FOR HITTING PRACTICE

Frequently a parent will ask how to help his child become a better ballplayer. We would reply, "Pitch to him so he can get more batting practice." Of all the drills on the basics of playing baseball, the drill that receives the least time *per player* is hitting, and the reason is understandable. If you have only one backstop and field, you can have only one batter hitting at a time, and if you give each player on a 12-player roster five minutes of hitting practice, you will consume an hour of practice time, during which time the other 11 players are idle.

Personal Attention

Compare that to a parent pitching for an hour; the child will get 12 times the amount of practice in hitting that's available in an average team practice. We recommend you have a bucket of balls available to lend to a parent willing to devote the extra time. The parent merely pitches them to the child, and then they will take a break as they retrieve the balls and start the sequence over again.

You will see more dramatic improvement in hitting than in any other practice drill in Little League with parent/child hitting practice. Could two kids achieve the same thing, practicing together, or could an older brother do the pitching? Theoretically, yes, but practice requires a certain discipline, particularly when it gets a little boring. Parents and coaches can impose the discipline more effectively than peers can.

Unfortunately some parents endure the frustration of watching their child strike out, time after time, and ask for help when the season is half over. Consequently, at the preseason registration parent meeting we encourage parents to practice with their children.

With respect to hitting in particular, we warn parents of the frustration that a rookie player feels—and that they will feel if their child consistently does poorly at the plate. Some rookies have gone through *an entire season without hitting the ball once in a game*, not only failing to get a hit but failing to hit the ball. Tell them how a few evenings of having someone pitch a bucket of balls might have helped those rookies.

As a coach, you naturally have to recognize situations where it is impossible for the parent-child pitching/hitting practice to take place—for example, parents' work schedules or parents' lack of coordination. A coach must be aware of those situations, so he can pair off those players with others whose parents may be willing to pitch to two kids; or you as coach may have to serve as a surrogate parent to give those kids some extra practice. There may be others—grandparents, neighbors, or even friends of the family—who might be willing to fill that role. If you encourage a player in that situation to "recruit" such a person, you may end up with a gem. Usually it will be the adult who brings the player to practice and stays to watch or always comes early.

The Basics

Batting drills don't require a ball field. They require only a wall or fence to hit into, and an area reasonably free of obstructions. Even in confined areas, a lot of hitting practice can be achieved from the "coach" tossing the ball underhand from the side and the batter hitting it into a fence or wall (see Figure 2.1). Even an uncoordinated parent can master that.

Hitting drills per se are not enough if the players and parents aren't practicing the basics of hitting. In fact, they can be harmful if the parent allows a player to repeat bad batting habits. Consequently, it is important that the parents, as well as the coaches, understand the basics of hitting that must be taught and then made mandatory in hitting drills.

2.1 Hitting Drill: A coach tosses a ball in from the side and a batter hits it into the fence.

Figures 2.2, 2.3, and 2.4 show a total of 31 checkpoints of hitting in the four-stage sequence. That might look intimidating, but every coach must know them, because it may be the failure to execute just one of them that will cause a strikeout instead of a hit. Even a major-league player in a batting slump will have his hitting coach analyze his swing (via sophisticated videotaping in slow motion) and may discover that carelessness in one of the 31 checkpoints is the cause of his hitting problems.

Since we advocate keeping it simple and making it fun, we recommend initially combining the 31 checkpoints into fewer basics for a coach to check. Mike Powers, Little League coach in St. Matthews, Kentucky, breaks the basics of hitting into just three checkpoints:

- The legs
- The head
- The timing

2.2 Ready!

2.3 Aim!

We call the three stages "ready, aim, fire," as shown in the following sequence.

Ready!

1. Bat is still.
2. Head is still.
3. Chin is on shoulder.
4. Shoulders are level.
5. Arms are parallel to ground.
6. Bat stays away from body.
7. Fingers are loose.
8. Knees are bent slightly.
9. Toes are on parallel line.
10. Front foot pivots toward pitcher.
11. Weight starts to shift to rear foot.
12. Arms move back.

Aim!

13. Eyes stay on ball.
14. Bat starts forward.
15. Front foot starts stride.
16. Knees turn inward.
17. Head remains still.
18. Wrists bring bat to level swing.

Fire!

19. Eyes watch ball hit bat.
20. Wrists snap at impact.
21. Weight shifts to front foot.
22. Swing is level.

2.4 Fire!

23. Shoulders are rounded.
24. Hips shift.
25. Rear knee bends.
26. Rear foot pivots.
27. Back toe remains on ground.
28. Wrists roll after contact.
29. Head remains still.
30. Torso turns with bat.
31. Follow-through is smooth.

Basic 1: Checking the Legs

Just as in pitching, where the whole body must be involved, Mike concentrates on the movement of the legs to force the whole body into the act of hitting. During a good swing, the batter steps toward the pitcher with his front foot and pushes with his back foot to start turning his body. As his body turns, he straightens and braces his front leg in order to control his body movement when his arms and hands come into position to hit the ball.

Many Little League batters (and pitchers) use only their upper body—shoulders and arms. Big, strong players get away with it; they hit home runs and strike out batters without learning the best way to hit or pitch.

By using his legs to help his swing, a batter can swing the bat slower for more accuracy and put his body's weight into the movement to provide more power. The swing should be quickly developed to the point where the batter turns his shoulders and hips back and uses his legs to get the body to turn forward with a slow, strong motion (see Figure 2.5). The batter is using the big muscles of the legs, hips, and shoulders to pull his arms and hands into position to hit. This pulling action is more powerful and controlled than the pushing action of using the upper body alone.

2.5 The batter is using his legs to get the body to turn forward with a slow, strong motion.

21

To demonstrate the sequence of leg and body movement in a swing, Mike Powers uses a simple drill that a player can practice alone. Mike calls it the Texas two-step, and it is shown in Figure 2.6. The batter locks a bat in his arms behind his back, steps forward with his front foot (left foot on a right-hander), and rotates the back foot (on the ball of the foot) until the heel is pointing at the backstop (in relationship to home plate). The action with the back foot is like squashing a bug.

The first part of the drill (stepping toward the pitcher) is fairly natural to a batter, unless he is inclined to be a "parachutist" who bails out for fear the ball will hit him. The second part of the drill (pushing and grinding with the rear foot) is something kids have to be taught and drilled until it becomes just as natural for them. That's where the Texas two-step becomes an effective personal drill, because it is impossible to avoid getting the whole body into the act of swinging when a batter, with a bat locked in his arms behind him, steps forward with the front foot and pushes back and grinds with the back foot. Try it, and you will see that this works.

How often have you seen a major-league batter raise his hand as he comes to bat (to ask the umpire for time), and "dig a hole" for his back foot. You should remind the kids to look for this routine when they are watching a game on TV. With his strong legs, if a major leaguer didn't do that and attempted to step forward with his front foot and push back with his rear foot, he would end up doing an embarrassed split in full view of the fans. To push off with the rear foot, a batter needs something solid to push against, like the back of the hole he has just dug for his rear foot.

Mike Powers has his players use the Texas two-step routine both in practice and in games before they come to bat. A couple of times in the on-deck circle will remind a batter to use his legs to get his whole body into the act of hitting.

22

I mentioned the "parachutist" who wants to bail out of the batter's box to avoid being hit with a pitched ball. Each year, every Little League team will have at least one rookie with the problem. Shame on the coach who doesn't correct it!

If you have a player with this problem, there is no point in trying to teach anything else about batting until you correct the problem. So long as his concentration is on how to avoid being hit, he will not concentrate on anything else. Parents sometimes

2.6 The "Texas two-step" teaches a batter to use the legs and body in the swing.

look shocked when we use this drill to correct this problem, but we find it very effective. Lay a bat, parallel to the plate, behind him and warn him that if he tries to bail out and steps on that bat, he may break his leg. If he still bails out by stepping over the bat, lay down two or three bats, until his fear of breaking a leg becomes greater than the fear of getting hit with the ball (see Figure 2.7). Then he stands in the box, and you can start concen-

2.7 Bats on the ground behind the batter teach him to stride toward the pitcher and not "bail out."

trating on his stepping toward the pitcher with the front foot while pushing and grinding with the rear one. We have tackled the bailing out problem with many players, without one broken leg. The solution will not always be permanent, however. If any player actually gets hit painfully with a pitched ball, watch out for the tendency to bail out the next time he comes to bat.

Basic 2: Head Still, Eyes on the Ball

As a drill to demonstrate this basic, take the position as a batter and have the player you are teaching stand on the pitching mound, facing you. As you go through the motion of swinging at an imaginary ball, ask him to watch your head. Even though your arms, wrists, shoulders, torso, and feet move as you go through the motions of hitting, your head remains still. Only when you have hit the ball does your head turn to the right and focus on first base as you break for that base. (In the process, you are teaching him not to watch the batted ball, which could slow down his dash for first base.)

Then tell the player to pretend the emblem on the cap is the ball and to watch your eyes as you again go through the act of hitting. With a player of average size, the emblem on his cap will be in your strike zone and your eyes will be riveted on it as you swing through the imaginary ball. Have the player on the mound take your place at bat, and another player take his place. By pairing off the kids in this way, after you have shown them the drill, they can take turns in this pretend drill of hitting the ball, while you go up and down the line checking their form. Let them critique each other, too, because in spotting the mistakes teammates make, players will mentally correct that mistake in themselves.

Having a batter focus on the emblem of the cap of the "pretend pitcher" will help teach following the ball in from the pitcher, since the emblem is about the size of a baseball.

You can then expand this drill with the use of Wiffle balls. Have the pitcher move toward the plate to the point where he can throw a straight ball—one that doesn't drop. Then have the batter concentrate on tracking the ball with his eyes. First he focuses on the cap emblem to get the distance range, then as the pitcher goes into his windup, the batter should focus on the shoulder of the pitcher's pitching arm, since the pitched ball will be released from above that shoulder. As the ball is released, the batter needs to attach his eyes to the ball and track it all the way in. The head remains still; only the eyes move as they follow the ball.

Some major-league hitters, the first time at bat against a pitcher, will "take" the first pitch, even if it's a strike. It is a tracking exercise for them in concentrating on the pitching motion, the release spot where they pick up the ball, and the movement and speed of the ball. They will track the ball right into the catcher's mitt. Their eyes are recording all of this information, so they will be ready for the next pitch. You will hear baseball announcers comment on the "good eyes" of a particular hitter. He seldom strikes out and rarely goes for a bad pitch, because he has mastered the skill of tracking the ball with his eyes. The late Ted Williams, the last major-league player to bat over .400 in a season, gave credit to his tracking ability for his success. He concentrated so much on tracking a pitched ball that he claimed he could see the stitches on the ball.

Another drill to help a batter's tracking ability is to have him stand in the batter's box with a pitcher pitching and a catcher catching. Although he has a bat and wears a batting helmet, the batter only practices tracking the ball and calls out "ball" or "strike" as the ball approaches the plate. The catcher (or an umpire) can audit the calls, and if he is consistently calling them wrong, then he obviously has a problem in tracking the ball accurately.

When a parent is practicing with a child, the parent can go through all of these drills before actually starting to pitch. If, in the tracking drill, the batter calls balls and strikes accurately, he is then ready for some actual hitting practice. It is easy to tell if he is tracking the ball well in a hitting drill, because he will be hitting the "sweet spots," that is, the center of the fat part of the bat will be hitting the center of the ball.

A batter who is not tracking well will be hitting the ball down the handle of the bat, foul-tipping it, missing it, or taking strikes. If this is happening, he needs to go back to the tracking drill, without swinging the bat. Try cutting the toe out of a brightly colored sock and fitting the open-ended sock on the "hot spot" of the bat. Then the sound will indicate whether the ball is being hit with the fat part of the bat.

Basic 3: Timing

If the tracking is accurate, the batter will know if it's a ball or a strike; but if it's a strike, where does he meet the ball? The answer is out in front of the plate, and the batter must be made to understand that, since a logical assumption would be to hit the ball when

2.8 The pepper drill teaches the batter to hit the ball out front.

it's over the plate. How often have you called to a batter who took a called strike, "Hey, Joe, that ball was *over the plate*"?

Few batters in Little League swing too early; many, many swing too late. This may explain why there are so many strikeouts in Little League.

Timing is a mental factor. If the batter is going to meet the ball in front of the plate, then he must be able to start his swing soon enough so that it reaches its peak of speed and power as the ball arrives in front of the plate. Only practice will condition the perfect timing.

One of the best drills to teach how to hit the ball out front is "pepper," a fun drill that combines quickness of hitting and quickness of fielding (see Figure 2.8). Usually three infielders are spread out in a half circle and pitch the ball (at slow speed), as soon as it is fielded, back to the hitter. Since the ball is coming slowly, the batter can time his swing to hit the ball on the fat of the bat, out in front. The repetition of this hitting the ball out in front will condition the batter on timing all of his swings to meet the ball at that point.

Mike Powers gives this additional tip on timing: "When the pitcher turns his shoulder, the batter should turn his." The last thing the pitcher does in the windup, before coming toward the plate with the ball, is turn the shoulder toward the plate (left shoulder for a right-handed pitcher). That's the point at which the batter should be turning the shoulder (left shoulder for a right-handed batter) and getting set to come forward with the bat.

The Level Swing

A tape recorder at a batting drill would probably record the coach's words "level swing" many times. It is obviously what every coach wants batters to do. For a Little Leaguer, however, getting a bat that starts in a semivertical position into a level position, parallel to the ground, is more easily said than achieved. When you have told him that the strike zone is from armpits to knees, a vertical distance of several feet, the rookie would be excused for not understanding how he could execute a level swing in both the highest and lowest planes of the strike zone. Of course, the answer is that he must adjust the whole body, bending the knees, while keeping the shoulders and elbows level, so the swing will naturally be level.

A drill mentioned before, and shown in Figure 2.1, that will allow a coach (or parent) to audit a child's level swing is the drill where the coach tosses the ball from the side and the batter hits it into a fence. The coach should purposely toss the ball in at different heights within the strike zone to see whether the batter adjusts the body to allow for a level swing. This is also a good drill to practice hitting the ball in front of the plate, since the coach can control his throw to make sure it is in a plane that is in front of the plate.

Coaches differ in their opinions of position of the feet, elbows, shoulders, and hands of a batter waiting for the pitch, yet they all agree that a swing should be level (parallel to the ground). We recommend the "parallel in–parallel out" approach as the easiest to remember.

The 31 checkpoints noted in Figures 2.2 through 2.4 can be simplified into basics that kids can remember. The parallel rules are:

- *Toes on a line parallel to the plate.* That should mean the batter hits up the middle, which is a good place to hit the ball. Trying to teach a Little Leaguer how to position hits is expecting him to achieve a higher level of baseball prematurely.
- *Shoulders parallel.* Dipping the shoulders will move the head and make a level swing impossible.
- *Elbows parallel.* If elbows are level going into the swing, they are more likely to be level coming out of the swing.
- *Chin parallel to shoulders.* Touching the shoulder with the chin will keep it parallel and prevent the head from moving.
- *Arms parallel.* Arms should be parallel to the body and away from it before the swing; they should be parallel to the ground as they are extended in a level swing.

That may seem like an oversimplification of the batting swing, but the "parallels rule" is easy to remember—certainly easier than the 31 checkpoints. It is the coach's job to remember the 31 checkpoints, and once players have mastered the basics of hitting, to start refining the checkpoints in a gradual process of helping them to become better batters. If you teach average 9- or 10-year-old rookies just to make contact with the ball, you will have done your job as a coach. As they gain the confidence that they *can* hit the ball,

2.9 A coach checks the correct batting stance of a player.

they will be eager to learn the further steps that will make them good hitters.

Confidence

The biggest obstacle for a Little League batter to overcome in order to be a good hitter, is not learning the mechanics of a good swing but gaining self-confidence. Many beginning Little Leaguers have an exaggerated fear of the ball and a low estimate of their own ability.

It seems that Little League players gain their confidence all of a sudden. When they do gain confidence, it is like having a new hitter on the team. Almost immediately they begin to hit the ball twice as well as before, without learning anything new about the mechanics of the swing.

The biggest challenge for the Little League manager and coach is to help young players to gain confidence. In games you need to let them know that you support them and that all you expect is that they try hard. When they make a good play or get a hit, show your appreciation.

In practices you can help young players to be better able to deal with their fear of the ball, as well as teach them how not to tense up and be unable to swing at good pitches.

Mike Powers teaches three things to help batters overcome their exaggerated fear of the ball:

- Admit that they are afraid of the ball. They are not weak or alone because they are afraid of the ball. Everyone who plays baseball, including major leaguers, is afraid of being hit by the ball.
- Learn how to avoid being hit by a pitch. On an inside pitch that could hit the batter, the batter should continue turning

the shoulders back until he is facing away from the pitcher, lower the head, and fall to the ground. By turning this way he can only get hit in the buttocks or the back of the legs. (The batter should never turn to face the pitcher to avoid being hit.)

- The most important thing the batters can do to avoid being hit by a pitch is to keep their eyes on the ball by tracking it all the way from release to the bat. The human reflexes are amazing. It is rare for a ballplayer to get hurt when truly concentrating on the ball.

To help players avoid tensing up and taking good pitches, in addition to dealing with the fear of the ball, we teach the player to begin making slight movements. The basic idea is not to stand rigidly in the batter's box but to make continuous slight movements with each part of the body—shifting weight slightly from one leg to the other, making short turns with the hips and shoulders, and making short practice swings to keep arms and hands loose. We begin by suggesting that batters "stay loose" by moving a little while waiting for the pitch.

We also get them to start the swing early in order to be ready to hit when the pitch is a strike. We tell them to turn the shoulders back when the pitcher turns his shoulders back and to step when the pitcher steps. To practice this we start by throwing a Wiffle ball from a short distance, having them take batting practice from a coach who is pitching easy from a short distance, and gradually move toward hitting balls thrown at full speed.

With all batters, we refine these movements into the basic four steps of a good swing:

1. *Get loose.* While the pitcher is getting ready and starting his windup, the batter is making slight movements to keep loose and ready to fly into action. He moves his feet "inside his

shoes"—moving slightly back and forth (toward the pitcher) without lifting the balls of the feet, and raising and lowering his heels as he shifts his weight. His hips and shoulders turn back and forth slightly as his weight shifts. He makes short practice swings.

2. *See the target.* His eyes are preparing to track the ball. He looks at the letter on the pitcher's cap to get the distance, finds the top of the shoulder on the pitcher's throwing arm, and watches for the ball to be released. He locks his eyes on the pitch as soon as it is released.

3. *Prepare.* He has refined what he learned as a beginner to turn his shoulders back when the pitcher turns his shoulders. Now he waits until the ball is released before turning his shoulders back. In order to overcome inertia he moves the bat from his chest to the batter's slot, swinging in one smooth motion back and then through. As he turns his shoulders back, he steps with his front foot. On every pitch, he steps with his front foot, and his hips and shoulders are ready to start turning.

4. *Pull the trigger.* When he makes the decision to swing, he will maintain good eye contact with the ball and start his swing by grinding his back foot and feeling the pulling action of his body as his hands approach the area in front of the plate where he will make contact. To make contact with the ball, he brings his arms, his hands, and then the bat, through the hitting area. Then his head stays down as he follows through.

Bunting Drills

The best way to teach rookies confidence and help overcome the fear of being hit by a pitched ball is to teach them how to bunt. In the correct bunting position, with both toes pointing at the pitcher, the batter has a full view of the ball and is able to track it best (see

Figure 2.10). The bat should make contact with the ball in front of the plate, as explained earlier, and it is much easier to time this when bunting. The ball should hit the fat part of the bat, and this is also much easier to accomplish in bunting. And, of course, proper timing in contacting the ball with the bat is important.

Too often when a coach is trying to analyze a hitter's problems in a normal pitching/hitting drill, the action is too fast to pick up the problems. In bunting, this is much easier. The batter whose timing is off in bunting will have a timing problem in hitting; the batter who bails out when bunting will have a serious problem with fear of the ball, and so on. On the positive side, the batter who can consistently meet the ball when taught to bunt will gain the confidence that is so important in learning to be a hitter.

2.10 A bunter bends his knees to use the fat part of the bat on a ball that is coming in at knee level.

A simple bunting drill starts with two players facing each other about 20 feet apart, one the batter, the other the pitcher. The batter assumes the bunting position: toes in a line pointing toward the pitcher, knees slightly bent, hands up on the bat far enough to control its direction, and upper hand cupped behind the bat.

Have the pitcher start with underhand tosses until the hitter is bunting the ball back consistently. Then have the pitcher throw overhand, but at half speed. When they have mastered the drill, they will be playing a modified form of pepper and can have fun keeping count of how many times they can keep the ball in play. The players rotate positions so each has a turn at both positions.

Hitting Drills

One of the most effective hitting drills is the two-player drill illustrated in Figure 2.11. It requires only a backstop or a fence to hit against. One player or a coach tosses the ball in from the side, and the batter hits it into the fence. It is better done with two players so the coach can watch and analyze the batter's swing.

Another variation of this drill uses a table. The batter stands on the table facing the backstop, and the "pitcher," lying on the ground, throws the ball up in a vertical plane for the batter to hit. It teaches a batter balance, because batters who stride too far or swing off balance risk falling off the table. (Naturally, a coach should be standing by to prevent this.)

Drill with a Pitching Machine

If your league is fortunate enough to have a pitching machine, by all means use it. However, it does take away one important element in teaching kids to hit: tracking the ball and perfecting the timing from the pitcher's windup and release.

2.11 Two-player hitting drill

The pitching machine has the great advantage of throwing strikes consistently, so a batter can get many more chances to connect with the ball in a given period of time than against a live pitcher. With the machine, you can time the hitting practice sequence and be reasonably sure that every player gets an equal amount of time at bat.

Start the machine at a slow speed to let batters get the feel of hitting and gradually speed it up to the average speed of pitching in your league (probably never more than 50 m.p.h.). Don't be tempted to set the dials at anything but a fastball, because the speed required to effect a machine-made curve or other trick pitch is greater than Little Leaguers should be facing.

In the Berlin Rookie League, a pitching machine is used in games, and the coach operating the machine fakes a pitcher's release of the ball as he feeds the ball into the machine.

Drills with the Batting Tee

Batters like to feel the bat hitting the ball. Nothing improves their batting confidence more. Most rookies can connect with a ball that is sitting on top of a batting tee. Those who can't, have serious batting problems that will require some personal coaching.

When a batter hits the ball off the tee, the coach can check all of the basics: head still, level swing, good stride, and so on. Even bunting form can be checked (see Figure 2.12).

A fun drill, using the batting tee and combining hitting, baserunning, and fielding, is to have actual inter-squad games with the batting tee. The players will enjoy this kind of practice, because there is lots of action and some competition.

36

2.12 One-player hitting drill off tee

Pitching/Hitting Drills

There's nothing like the real thing. A coach can pitch in hitting drills, and the temptation is great, since he will have better control, but it isn't the real thing unless you have a coach who is the same size as a Little Leaguer and pitches at the same speed.

To make it good practice for pitchers as well as hitters, we make the first pitcher warm up well before the session starts and have a second pitcher warming up to take his place after every five batters (the average number of batters a Little League pitcher faces in an inning).

Many coaches will tell a batter in a pitching/hitting drill to bunt three and hit three. But that isn't the real thing. Have them take a turn at bat, with an umpire calling balls and strikes, and either hit the ball, strike out, or walk. To avoid wasting time with horseplay on the bases, the batter goes as far as he can go if he hits the ball, but then comes back to the dugout and gets in line to hit again. The practice will move much faster and will confine itself to pitching, hitting, and fielding. You can expand it at another time to become a full practice session, involving stealing and baserunning, but if your objective is to provide the maximum real-thing batting drill, then let the kids just keep coming to the plate and encountering the same situation they will have every time they come to bat in a game. If they get used to the real thing, they will be more relaxed when it happens in a game.

3

DRILLS FOR PITCHING PRACTICE

Grooming an effective pitching staff can be a challenging task. It is important to train at least four pitchers to be eligible to pitch at any time. Good drafting can make your job easier, but the obviously good pitchers will be spread evenly throughout the league. You will need to train some players who have had little pitching experience. Make this a priority! Without enough dependable pitchers, it may turn into a long, frustrating season.

In team practice, coaches often face the problem that they can work with only one player at a time. For that reason we try to find a pitching coach who spends all of his time, in every practice, working with the pitchers one at a time. Unless he is willing to be the catcher in these pitching drills, which is a physically demanding assignment, he will have to have some help, either from another parent/coach or from catching prospects on the team.

Your best pitcher, if you have a good defensive team, will always be the one who can put pitches in the strike zone the greatest percentage of the time. He needn't have a blazing fastball, or change-up, or curve—just a ball of any description that finds the strike zone.

Choosing Your Pitchers

During preseason practice, have your potential pitchers pitch 20 times and see who pitches the most strikes. Give every player the opportunity to try out for pitcher. Sometimes the player you initially overlook will surprise you. But don't just use this drill once; use it on successive days, keeping the cumulative stats of balls and strikes thrown. It will provide the pitchers with competition and incentive to practice on their own, keeping their own ball/strike statistics, until they can consistently throw in the strike zone. It will also sort out for you the players with a casual interest in pitching from those who are dedicated. The latter group will go through their pitching drills every day, and not just during team practice.

Ideally you should have two 12-year-olds (the maximum you can use in a week, per Little League rules), two 11-year-olds, and two 10-year-olds as potential pitchers. Practically speaking, however, you can't give six pitchers enough work to sharpen their pitching skills if you play only two games each week. So we recommend concentrating on your four best pitchers, so long as only two are 12-year-olds.

You may get into the frustrating situation of having three 12-year-old pitchers of nearly equal ability as the season begins. If you also have a good 11-year-old pitcher, it makes the problem even more frustrating, since he will get less pitching time if you elect to alternate your three 12-year-olds, with one having to skip every third week. Our recommendation is to get the kids and their parents together in the preseason and explain that the Little League rules prevent your using more than two 12-year-old pitchers in a week, so you must narrow down the choice to two and will do it in the fairest way possible: by comparing their statistics (walks, hits, runs, strikeouts, fielding errors, etc.) in preseason practice games. Schedule as many preseason practice games as possible and work the three 12-year-olds until you can reach a decision. The child not selected, and the parents, will understand why and how the decision was made. It will avoid morale-harming dissension on the part of a parent who assumes the child was discriminated against.

One other basic rule in choosing your pitchers: choose the big kids. Since you won't have the device the major-league teams have to measure the speed of a fastball, you have to assume that the bigger they are, the faster they pitch. You can teach a big pitcher control, but you can't teach a small pitcher speed. This may seem to contradict our earlier statement that the best pitcher is the one who has the best control. We'll still stand by that statement, but if you have to choose between two pitchers with equal control, pick the big one.

Pitching Drills

The drill for choosing pitchers (keeping cumulative totals of strikes and balls thrown in practice) should be continued after your pitchers are chosen, because now you have to rank your chosen pitchers on dependability. Keep daily records to measure their progress. Then start keeping a record of strike position, differentiating between a low strike (belt to knees) and a high strike (belt to armpits).

It is well known that a low pitch is more desirable for these two basic reasons: (1) It is harder to hit; and (2) if hit, it will usually result in a ground ball.

There's the old joke about the stranger in New York City who asked someone, "How do you get to Carnegie Hall?" The answer was "Practice, practice, practice!" A coach of mine paraphrased it to "How do you get to be a good ballplayer?" with the same answer.

There is no position in baseball where daily practice is more important in sharpening a player's skills than the pitching position.

You hear of a pitcher's rhythm, and it is particularly important to a Little League pitcher, awkward about pivoting on a pitcher's rubber, to develop a rhythm that becomes comfortable and automatic. Have you ever seen a bullpen in a major-league park without two pitching rubbers—one for the right-handed relief pitcher and one for the lefty? If just throwing the ball were the only important part of warming up, then the practice rubber would be superfluous. In fact, the whole process of winding up, pivoting the front foot on the rubber, pushing off the rubber, and following through is basic to the pitching rhythm.

Does your Little League ballpark have any practice pitching rubbers? If not, you are not providing your pitchers with one of the necessary tools for pitching drills. If the infield is being used for fielding or batting practice, then your pitchers obviously cannot use the regular pitching rubber for their drills. The four parts of a pitcher's rhythm that must be developed are shown in Figures 3.1 through 3.5.

Mike Powers teaches his pitchers to practice their rhythm even when they are passing the ball to loosen up for practice. He breaks down the four parts of the pitching motion as follows:

1. *Extend and raise the throwing arm.* Have the player catch the ball and turn sideways. Then he puts his throwing hand in the glove and moves his hands toward his chest. As his hands get to his chest, he takes the ball out of the glove and extends and raises his throwing arm. Tell him to reach for the center-field flag, "long-arming" (or making the arm "long" before throwing the ball).

2. *Step with the left foot.* Instruct the pitcher to keep his left knee bent and to land on the ball of his foot. Also have him point the toes of his left foot toward the target. After he learns to do this, draw two interconnecting lines in the dirt. One line is the size of the pitching rubber, and the other is a

straight line from the middle of the pitching rubber toward the target. Have the pitcher place his right foot on the right side of the pitching rubber and then land with his left foot on the line that was drawn toward the target.

3. *Push off the rubber.* This movement involves rotating on the ball of the right foot and then pushing the weight forward with the toes. Teach this movement by having the pitcher compare rotating on the ball of the foot to squashing a bug on the sidewalk. The pitcher grinds the ball of the foot and then pushes his weight forward with his toes.

4. *Lean forward.* Explain that the pitcher needs to lean forward to throw a low strike. Have him stand sideways to the target, spread his feet and bend his knees, and extend and raise his throwing arm. Then he does only two things to throw: He pushes off the rubber and leans forward.

3.1 Pitcher starts his windup.

3.2 The rubber foot pivots as he finishes his windup.

3.3 The whole body is involved as the front leg comes up and the back bends.

3.4 The front foot strides, the rear foot pushes off the rubber, the back is bent, and the ball is thrown "from center field."

After the pitcher learns these basic movements, he can pitch from the mound. He now understands the important movements of the delivery and will be able to appreciate why he needs to make a correct windup. Then you can teach him the full sequence of the pitch from the stance to the fielding position.

Balance is very important to a pitcher's rhythm. There are three points in the delivery

3.5 The rear foot comes forward to assume a fielding position to complete the follow-through.

where balancing drills can be
helpful:

1. *The flamingo.* This is Mike
   Powers's term to make the
   analogy between standing
   on the pivot leg with the
   other knee raised waist high
   in the position of the
   flamingo, standing perfectly
   balanced on one leg. Having your pitchers practice
   being flamingos will help
   them with this important
   balance phase of pitching (see Figure 3.6).

3.6 Here is an
example of
"flamingo"
position in a
pitcher's delivery.
His body is
perfectly
balanced on his
pivot leg.

2. *The sitting position.* This is when the left knee (on a right-
   handed pitcher) is raised and the arm is going back toward
   center field. At this point the pitcher should bend his right
   knee to get his body in a lowered position—like he is sitting
   down.

3. *Using the back.* You will hear coaches admonishing their
   pitchers to "use your back" or "use your body"—as opposed
   to just pitching with the arm. If you see this weakness in a
   pitcher, have another player hold his pivot foot as he comes
   around. There is no way, with this restriction, that he can
   pitch the ball without bending his back and following
   through. Figure 3.7 shows this drill being used on a right-
   handed pitcher.

Pitcher as Fielder

You have little to fear as long as your pitcher is pitching consistently
in the strike zone and you have a good infield.

3.7 Holding the pitcher's rear foot in practice drill forces him to use his whole body.

You often hear the phrase "a good infield backing up the pitcher," but in fact *the pitcher is part of the infield*. So if your pitcher is not a good fielder, you do not have a good infield. A savvy coach of an opposing team will notice a pitcher who is off balance when he finishes pitches, and will have his team bunt. Nothing will unnerve a team (or a coach) more than to have the batter hit an easy bounce back to the pitcher and then have the pitcher throw the ball three feet over the first baseman's head.

Figure 3.8 shows a drill for pitchers learning how to cover first base on a grounder to the first baseman. In the drill, you line up your pitchers on the mound and let them take turns circling to the inside of the base and taking the underhand throw from the first baseman. If you have more than one first baseman, you can rotate at that position, too, as the coach hits grounders to the first-base position.

A good fielding drill for a pitcher—involving pitcher, catcher, and first baseman—is this: Have the pitcher pitch as he normally would, and have the catcher throw grounders to the left of the mound, or to the right, or directly back (but in no sequence, so the pitcher will not know where the ball is coming). Have the pitcher field the ball and throw to first.

Another fielding drill, involving the same three players, is to have the catcher throw a ball to the right side, out of reach of the pitcher, which the first baseman must field, and have the pitcher cover first. It is important to teach the pitcher to circle back into the infield when he touches first, in order to avoid a collision with the base runner, who is running up the line on the foul side of the first-base line (see Figure 3.9).

For variation and to add some reality to the play, add a runner to these drills.

When teaching the "hot-box" drill outlined in Chapter 5, note that *the pitcher is involved as a fielder in every hot-box situation.* He backs up the first baseman in a rundown between first and second, backs up the third baseman in a rundown between second and third, and backs up the catcher in a rundown between third and home.

A pitcher who does not cover home on a wild pitch or passed ball will make stealing home easy for the opposition. A savvy coach will notice that the pitcher is not covering and tell the base runners to take advantage of the situation. If you see a new opposing pitcher enter the game when you have a runner on third, signal that runner to go far off base on every pitch, because a new pitcher is likely to be wild and to be too nervous to remember to cover home on a wild pitch or passed ball.

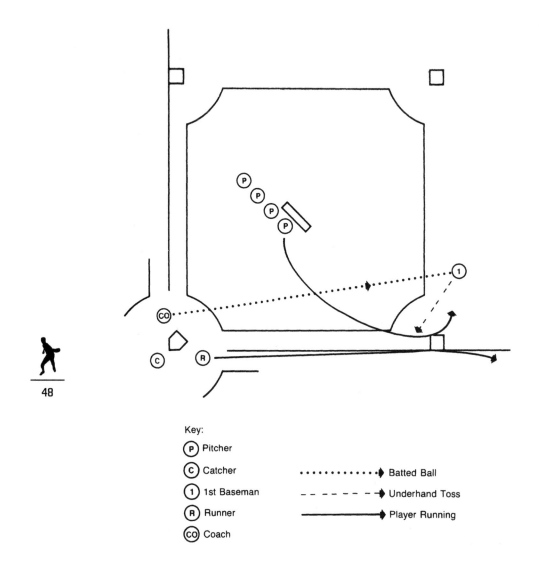

48

Key:

(P) Pitcher

(C) Catcher ••••••••••••▶ Batted Ball

(1) 1st Baseman – – – – – –▶ Underhand Toss

(R) Runner ─────────▶ Player Running

(CO) Coach

3.8 Pitcher covering first base drill

To add another dimension to your pitcher's fielding ability, you can add a runner on third to either of the two drills. Either the pitcher will naturally throw some wild pitches, or the catcher will

3.9 The first baseman (left) has tossed the ball underhanded to the pitcher (center), who has touched the base and is circling back to the infield to avoid colliding with the runner (right).

deliberately let some balls pass to drill the pitcher's ability to do three difficult fielding maneuvers:

1. Cover home plate.
2. Take the throw from the catcher.
3. Tag the runner without dropping the ball.

It is frustrating to see steps 1 and 2 executed, only to have the pitcher fail at step 3. It obviously merits some drilling. How often have you seen a batter walk, steal second, go to third on a wild pitch, and steal home on a passed ball? It happens so often in our league that we figure two out of three walks are automatic runs. Now do you understand why control is so important in pitchers?

50

3.10 Two ways to grip the fastball

How Many Pitches?

So far, the only pitch discussed has been the fastball. Until a pitcher has mastered rhythm and control, don't consider teaching any advanced pitches. However, after your pitcher has learned control, you can teach him variations of the fastball by adjusting his grip. He can either cross the stitches with his fingers or let them run parallel to the stitches (see Figure 3.10). Have your pitchers practice both ways, and observe the difference in delivery, if any. Sometimes the cross-stitch grip, coupled with a wrist snap at the release, will cause the ball to tail off like a curveball.

When your pitcher has mastered the fastball, consider teaching more advanced pitches. The following coaching tips on breaking pitches give special consideration to avoiding pitching deliveries that could hurt a young pitcher's arm.

Breaking Pitches

There are three basic types of breaking pitches: (1) the slider, which breaks horizontally; (2) the sinker, which breaks vertically; and (3) the curve, which breaks horizontally and vertically simultaneously. Depending on a batter's swing pattern (which every pitcher should pay attention to when choosing both pitch and location), one breaking pitch may be more effective than another. For example, a slider (horizontal break) is theoretically a more difficult pitch for a batter whose swing is vertical (that is, the tip of the bat travels up-to-down or down-to-up during the swing). Conversely, a sinker would be a more difficult pitch for a batter with a horizontal swing (that is, the tip of the bat travels laterally or parallel to the ground during the swing). In general, we believe the most effective breaking pitch is a curveball, as it compromises both the basic swing patterns.

There are two forces that cause a baseball to change direction: spin, or rotation, and gravity. Rotation can be accomplished in three ways: by grip, by grip pressure, or by the sudden rotation or twisting of the wrist at the moment of release of the ball. Little League players should not be taught or encouraged to use this third method; it should be taught only to older players whose arms are more developed, as repeated use of this pitch can damage a pitcher's arm. Hence, only a static release without the snapping of the wrist will be explained here.

Grip

The pitcher should grip the seams of the baseball to exaggerate the desired rotation; the faster the rotation relative to the velocity of the ball, the more the pitch will break. For maximum rotation, the index and middle fingers should be kept together as the baseball is gripped along the ridge of a seam. (The different breaking pitches will be described from a right-handed perspective). The position of the fingers at the point of release ranges from the index and middle fingers at 12 o'clock and the thumb at 6 o'clock to the index and middle fingers at 3 o'clock and the thumb at 9 o'clock. The latter pitch is much like a forward spiral pass in football. *Do not* teach your pitcher to violently twist or snap the wrist at the point of release—it is not necessary! A 1 o'clock release will get more of a sliding action (horizontal break) on the ball with less velocity, similar to a change-up. A 2 o'clock release will put more of a curving action on the ball. The beauty of these pitches is that the delivery is the same motion as that of the fastball; hence, the pitcher does not telegraph the pitches to the batter. Keep in mind that velocity, grip pressure, and varying seam locations alter the kind of break your pitcher ultimately produces. It is worth your time and energy to have your pitchers experiment with the different combinations of grip, grip pressure, seam location, and velocity to produce the most effective pitch.

Grip Pressure

There are subtle differences in how each pitcher grips and releases a baseball. Encourage your pitchers to experiment with different grip pressures along different seam variations so that they can discover and develop their own unique and most effective delivery. For example, with the index and middle fingers together, applying more pressure with the middle finger against a seam will naturally impart greater spin or rotation on the ball at the point of release. However, doing this may make the ball more difficult to control at first; mastery of this pitch usually requires a great deal of practice.

In general, the greater the velocity, the later the breaking action occurs. Thus, the speed at which a breaking pitch is thrown is very important in how and when it breaks. Ideally, breaking pitches should break just in front of the hitting zone. Keep in mind that merely changing the speed of the pitch (e.g., a change-up) can be effective in confusing a batter. Pitchers should experiment with the right velocity to see how it affects their curveball.

Release

The release is the most crucial, yet simplest, element of throwing a breaking pitch. Normally, when throwing a curveball, the pitcher violently snaps the wrist at the point of release to impart spin to the baseball, causing it to curve. Unfortunately, this snapping action, as mentioned earlier, causes undue stress and strain on the arm and, over time, can often cause chronic arm, elbow and/or shoulder problems, not to mention a career-ending injury. Also, the surprise effect of the pitch is greatly compromised by this snapping action, because the upward movement of the elbow thereby telegraphs the pitch.

We prefer a "static" release, as opposed to a "kinetic" release; that is, rather than violently snapping the wrist and arm at the point of release, the pitcher should maintain the wrist in a fixed position and throw the ball much the same way a quarterback would throw a spiral pass with a football. With experimentation and practice a pitcher can master effective and safe breaking pitches that will preserve the pitching arm, not injure it.

The Chopping Curveball

One simple pitch is the "chopping" curveball (see Figure 3.11). The ball should be held on the seams with the two-finger grip. The middle finger should hold the ball tight and the index finger should only stabilize the ball. When thrown, the ball should roll over the index finger and get some snap from the middle finger. The motion of the wrist should be like chopping with a hatchet. When the ball is released, the hand should look like a finger gun. This pitch does not impact the arm as severely as the classic curve does, but it can move the ball just as much. As always, only practice will make this an effective pitch. We suggest that only fast balls be thrown until the count favors a curveball. An 0-2 or 1-2 count is the best, since the pitcher is ahead of the batter and can come back with a fastball if the curve does not get an out. The choice of pitch should be left up to the coach and communicated to the pitcher and catcher through a predetermined signal.

54

3.11 Note the height of the ball and the pitcher's follow-through while throwing a "chopping curveball."

Change-Ups

Changing the speed of the ball as it crosses the plate can get the same results as a curveball with less risk of a passed ball or wild pitch. We use two different change-up pitches. The first is called the "circle" change. The pitcher should make a circle with his thumb and forefinger, as if making the OK sign. That circle should be placed on the ball so that the index and middle fingers grip the laces, as if throwing a curveball. The remaining two fingers should grip the ball to complete a palm grip. This pitch should be thrown just like a fastball. The different grip will cause the ball to be released from the hand more slowly and result in less velocity.

The other change-up is the "Vulcan" change. This pitch is rather difficult to master, but it can result in slower velocity and even a tail on the ball as it crosses the plate. The Vulcan change is gripped as shown in Figure 3.12; it is thrown exactly like the fastball, except that upon release the pitcher rotates the wrist counterclockwise to

3.12 Three breaking-ball grips: (from left) the "Vulcan change-up," the "chopping curveball," and the "circle change-up"

allow the ball to roll off the hand backward. This pitch is more difficult to master than the curve, but it is very effective.

A really serious young pitcher who is willing to practice and perfect breaking pitches is well advised to consider baseball camps and/or training centers operated by professionals. Most of these camps have qualified coaches who can oversee pitching workouts and supervise pitchers' development.

4

DRILLS FOR DEFENSIVE PRACTICE

In the preceding chapter, we recommended giving all players a chance to show you what they have so you do not overlook a good prospect. This is true not just of the new rookies, but of the returning players as well. If you predetermine a child's capabilities based on what she did last year, you aren't allowing for the tremendous changes that can occur in a year in size, speed, strength, and coordination. Giving everyone a chance to play every position is important in your early-season practices.

Tryout Drill

Give all the players at least one opportunity to try out as a pitcher, catcher, first baseman (record the distance they can stretch from their glove to the bag), infielder, and outfielder.

Baserunning Drill

You need to know how fast players are so that you will know how to coach them as base runners. Using a stopwatch, record their speed from home to first, in stealing second, and in circling the bases. Rather than racing the players against each other, which embarrasses the slower ones, keep an individual record on each player and encourage him to beat his best time in subsequent time trials.

Aim for "Strong Up the Middle"

The backbone of your defense has to be the up-the-middle positions: catcher, pitcher, second baseman, shortstop, and center fielder. They should be your strongest, fastest, best-coordinated kids. And they should be the positions where you substitute the least, in order to maintain a strong up-the-middle defense.

Frequently your best pitchers will also be your best shortstops, so if you alternate at that position, it will mean the least disruption of your up-the-middle defense. Your best pitchers may also be good catchers, but since the position of catcher is most prone to injury and is physically demanding, it is better to avoid using pitchers in the catching position. I have seen players catch for three innings on a hot day and then be asked to pitch. They obviously won't be at peak strength after three perspiring innings behind the plate.

Around-the-Horn Drill

Around the horn is a good drill for giving all players a chance to practice at every position. Ideally you should have three coaches, plus yourself, conducting the drill, which allows everyone to practice at the same time and prevents boredom on the part of watchers. Figure 4.1 shows how your coaches would line up: one between home and third, hitting grounders to the first and second basemen and fly balls to the right fielder and right-center fielder; another coach between home and first base, hitting grounders to the third baseman and shortstop and fly balls to the left fielder and left-center fielder; and a third coach behind home plate, working with the pitchers and catchers. However, it is more desirable to have the pitchers and catchers move to another field, if possible. If you are free of any coaching responsibility in this drill, you will have the

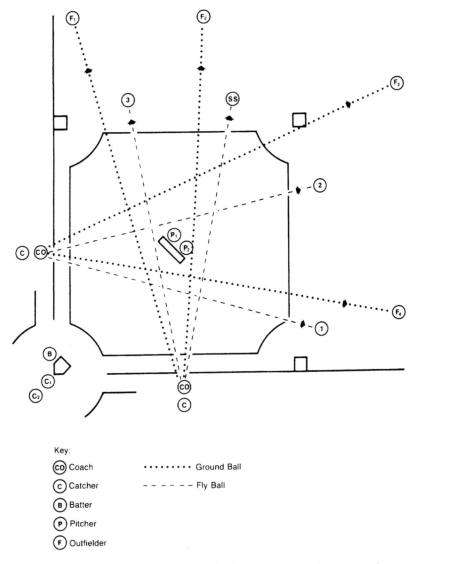

Key:

(co) Coach	•••••••• Ground Ball
(c) Catcher	− − − − − − Fly Ball
(B) Batter	
(P) Pitcher	
(F) Outfielder	

4.1 Around-the-horn practice routine (using as many as three coaches and 15 players)

opportunity to take notes on the performance of each player at each position.

To enable everyone to play every position, rotate the players periodically in the course of the drill. Note that there are 15 positions to hold (including the "pretend batter" working with the pitchers and catchers).

The normal shift in rotating the players is from left to right. To shift from outfield to infield, the sequence is right fielder to catcher (helping the coach between home and first) to third base. To shift from infield to outfield, the sequence is from first baseman to catcher (helping the coach between home and third) to left field.

When evaluating infielders, check:

- Reaction time in moving to the position of the grounder
- Ability to field the ball
- Speed in getting rid of the ball
- Ability to catch the relay from an outfielder
- Speed and accuracy in throwing to the catcher

Recognizing that this is an early practice drill, you don't expect perfection, but you look for the raw talent that is coachable and the basic weaknesses that may not be easily coachable, such as fear of the batted ball.

In evaluating outfielders, check:

- Reaction time in going to the position of the fly ball
- Ability to position themselves accurately
- Ability to catch the ball
- Speed in getting rid of the ball
- Speed and accuracy in throwing to the relay

Boredom of players in practice is a serious problem for coaches. Young players will quit your team if they are bored and have something more interesting to do. This drill is a great way to prevent boredom, since all players are active and there is variety in what they are practicing.

It should be noted that in preventing boredom by having different things going on to involve all of your players at the same time, there is an obvious risk of injury if the various drills are not well organized and kept as far apart as possible. The around-the-horn drill requires the services of three adult coaches at the same time, and as a safety consideration should not be conducted with any fewer. The same precautions should be exercised in any drills where more than one ball and bat are used at the same time.

Avoid Stereotypes

The stereotypes of the big catcher and the big, left-handed, clumsy first baseman are unfortunate. Since the catcher is one of the key players in the up-the-middle defense, you don't want a big, clumsy player in that position. Some of the best catchers are small, quick, "good head" players. Many major-league teams relegate good hit–poor field players to the first-base position, because plays at first base are so routine. Nothing is routine in Little League, however, and since a much bigger percentage of balls are hit to the right side of the diamond, your first baseman needs to be a good fielder and well-coordinated. It takes a lot of footwork to touch the base and catch a ball at the same time.

Why are many balls hit to the right side of the infield? Because inexperienced batters often swing late on fastballs. The advantage of being left-handed is not as great in Little League as in higher levels of baseball, so don't put a player at first base just because he is left-handed. On the other hand, first base is the best position for a good infielder, since the other infield positions favor right-handed throwers.

The tendency of coaches in early season is to go immediately to the traditional infield drills of hitting to the infielder, who throws to first; hitting to the infielder, who throws to the catcher; double play; and the like. There will be plenty of time for that later. Initially, however, you should spend a lot of time on the around-the-horn drill to evaluate your team's varied talents. Rotate the players frequently, since a lot of throwing is involved and you will get sore-arm complaints if you let the drill continue too long. When you have established which kids will play infield and which will play outfield, you can then break your defensive practices into three groups: infielders, outfielders, and pitchers/catchers, preferably with a coach for each group, so that you can roam among all three.

Fielding Technique

It is important initially to establish the correct "set" position for an infielder as the pitcher delivers and emphasize this position for every pitch.

- Feet spread wider than shoulder width
- Balanced on balls of the feet and able to shift weight from side to side
- Legs bent and butt low
- Hands on knees until pitcher winds up; then hands out, knee-high
- Eyes on the strike zone as pitcher releases the ball

When the ball is hit in their fielding area, infielders must:

1. Move to the ball, charging it if it is a slow roller, or moving to the spot of intercept (see Figure 4.2)

2. Keep the body low in order to keep the glove low, since the most common infielding error is letting the ball go under the glove

3. Keep the eyes on the ball and "look it into the glove" (see Figure 4.3)

4. Pick the ball out of the glove and sight on the target (see Figure 4.4)

5. Step toward the target while throwing (see Figure 4.5)

An infielder's biggest fear is getting hit in the face with a "bad hop." To help overcome this fear and protect against the bad hop, Mike Powers recommends holding the bare hand above the glove, palm down, to be ready to stop the bad bounce. It's an excellent tip, because infielders who get hit in the face with a ground ball are

4.2 The shortstop moves to the ball.

4.3 He looks the ball into his glove.

4.4 He picks the ball out of his glove and gets a fix on the target.

4.5 He steps toward the target (first base) as he throws.

most likely going to be "gun-shy" on hard-hit grounders until they forget the hurt.

Good infielders will show aggressiveness in fielding the ball and will go after it instead of waiting for it to come to them. It is what coaches call playing the ball and not letting the ball play you. It is part instinct, part training. Players who are aggressive in other ways are also aggressive infielders, and the reverse is also true. The player who demonstrates a fear of being hit at bat and is always bailing out will normally carry that fear onto the field and will be difficult to coach into becoming a good infielder.

A symptom of fear of getting hit is "side-saddling" the ball—trying to field the grounder by reaching to the side, instead of in front of the body. It is safe, from an injury standpoint, since if the ball takes a bad hop, it will bounce over the glove into the outfield.

But it's bad fielding technique, because a bad hop that the body blocks can still be an out or save a run, but a bad bounce over the glove is a hit and possibly an RBI.

Infield Drills

To teach the basics of the technique of fielding an infield ball, we advocate, two-, three-, or four-player drills before going to the standard drill of the coach hitting grounders and the infielder throwing to first. That drill is important, but it should be preceded in the early practices of the season with more basic, individualized instruction with drills such as the ones that follow.

The "Alligator"

Mike Powers's invention to teach players to keep their bare hand above the glove with palm down is called the "alligator." It helps in three ways:

- It protects against the bad hop.
- It secures the catch by clamping the bare hand on the ball in the glove.
- It helps a quick release as the fielder digs the ball out of the glove for the throw.

The reason Mike calls it the "alligator" is that it looks like the jaws of an alligator clamping down on the ball. The analogy helps kids remember the proper technique (see Figure 4.6).

It is a two-person drill, with one player being the infielder, the other the first baseman. The coach rolls the ball to the infielder, who fields it and makes the throw to the first baseman. At first the coach throws slow rollers directly to the infielder; then he increases speed and varies location.

4.6 The right hand is above the glove, palm down like an alligator.

You can have as many players active in this drill as you have infield ground to use.

The Bouncing Ball

You hear baseball announcers talk about an infielder fielding a ball on the "high hop" or on the "short hop." These are the two ideal points at which to field a bouncing ball—when it is at its highest point or just as it starts to rise. Which way to play the ball is a split-second decision an infielder has to make as he sees the ball coming toward him "on the hop." Only practice will develop both the skill and the judgment necessary to make the play consistently.

In this two-player drill, one player is the infielder, the other the first baseman. The first baseman bounces the ball to the infielder, who fields it and throws to first.

The Dive

An infielder needs to be taught to make two kinds of dive catches: the line-drive catch and the bouncing-ball catch.

The dive drill is either a two-player or three-player drill. In the three-player drill, two infielders can be playing the shortstop and second base positions, and the third player or coach stands between the pitcher's rubber and second base. The third player alternates line-drive throws or bouncing balls to either side of the two infielders, enough out of their reach that they have to dive for them (see Figure 4.7). This is a catching version of the "pepper drill," which is described next, in that part of the drill involves the infielder releasing the ball as quickly as he can back to the thrower. It is a fast-paced drill, guaranteed to tire your participants quickly.

If your infield is very hard, it is better to have the infielders playing back at the edge of the outfield grass, so their dives are cush-

4.7 The coach throws a ball out of reach of the infielders, who must dive for it.

ioned by the grass. This, like a sliding drill, is better done after some rain when the infield is soft. However, to prepare for all infield conditions, all infield drills should be done on varying surfaces to demonstrate the different ways a ball bounces, depending on soft or hard infields. Even major-league controversies have occurred in which one team has accused another of having either too hard or too soft a surface. Our All-Star team has played on fields where the infield grass was so high and the infield surface was so soft that it was impossible for a ground ball to get through. The home team was used to playing under those conditions and had an advantage.

On one field, when we took our All-Star team to practice a day before the game, there appeared to be no pitcher's mound. There was a rubber, but it seemed to be level with home plate. We asked the home-field manager when they were going to construct the mound, and he told me rather indignantly that their pitcher's rubber was the Little League prescribed height above home plate and he had the surveyor's certification to prove it. Be that as it may, the fact remained that it had a different look and feel, which the home-team pitchers were used to but the visiting pitchers had difficulty adjusting to.

Pepper Drill

The pepper drill is a fun drill that your kids will enjoy. Usually it involves a batter and three infielders (see Figure 4.8), although it can be done with a batter and one infielder. The number of simultaneous drilling groups is limited only by the infield you have available. Even with only one infield, you could have as many as four drills going on simultaneously, as Figure 4.9 demonstrates. To avoid balls going through the batter and interfering with another group drilling, it is wise to have a catcher backing up each hitter. If you use all the players, you can have as many as 15 practicing at the same time. If you have fewer players, then have fewer infielders per group, which will give each player more balls to field. Naturally,

4.8 Pepper drill: batter and three infielders try to keep the ball in play.

you rotate your team members within each group so that all have a chance to field and hit.

The fielders throw the ball back to the batter overhand, but at half speed, and she hits the ball at half strength. The fun of the drill is in keeping the ball in play. To add some competition to the drill, challenge them to see which group can keep the ball in play the longest time. Have them count the number of hit balls before the sequence is broken.

This drill will give not only practice in quick-response fielding, but good eye-hand coordination practice in batting as well.

Standard Infield Drill

The standard infield drill of a coach hitting in sequence to his infielders is:

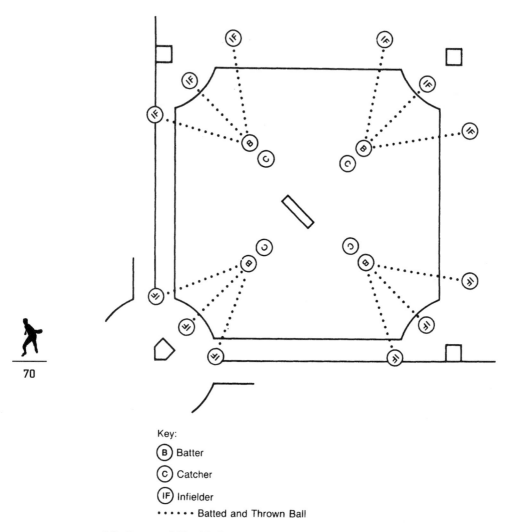

Key:
- (B) Batter
- (C) Catcher
- (IF) Infielder
- • • • • • Batted and Thrown Ball

4.9 Pepper drill with four groups on one infield

70

1. Throw back to catcher.
2. Throw to first and back to catcher.
3. One and cover: throw to first, back to catcher, catcher back to infielder covering her base.

4. Around the horn: throw to first, who throws to second, to short, to third, to home.

5. Force at second: throw to second baseman or shortstop covering second.

6. Force at third: throw to third baseman.

7. Force at home: throw to catcher.

A lot of coaches include a double-play drill, but how many double plays did you see in your league last year? And how many errors on an attempted double play? We would rather concentrate on the force-play drill and not complicate it with the pivot and throw to first to attempt the double play. Remember that the baselines in Little League are only 60 feet, versus 90 feet in higher levels of play, so it is an exceptionally slow runner who cannot beat out a double play.

Catching Pop-Ups

Figure 4.10 shows the areas in which various infielders should catch pop-ups. You will note that the pitcher is excluded, and for good reason. He has the two problems of coming off the mound and being off balance to catch a pop-up, which just make the assignment more difficult. It is better to leave him out of it, since the smaller infield in Little League should allow the other five infielders to cover the designated areas easily.

I recommend that you lay down lines, as Figure 4.10 shows, so your infielders get used to understanding their designated areas for catching pop-ups. Nevertheless, there will be borderline cases where these rules should be applied:

• The fielder coming in should take it, rather than the fielder backing out (see Figure 4.11).

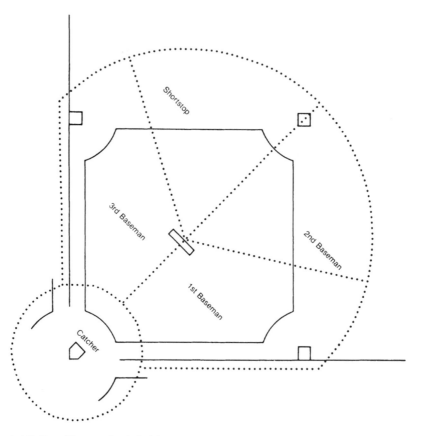

4.10 Pop flies to the infield

- The fielder who doesn't have to reach across her body should take it, rather than the fielder who does. Thus, with all right-handed infielders, a borderline pop-up between the first baseman and second baseman should be taken by the second baseman (see Figure 4.12); one between the second baseman and shortstop should be taken by the shortstop (see Figure 4.13); and one between the shortstop and third baseman should be taken by the third baseman.
- A backup fielder should always move into position to help the fielder making the catch (see Figure 4.14).

4.11 The center fielder, coming in, makes the catch rather than the shortstop, who is moving back.

4.12 On borderline plays between the first and second basemen, the second baseman should make the catch.

Naturally, the surest way to avoid collision is for the player who should catch the ball to call out "I've got it," or "Mine," and wave his arms to emphasize with movement (in case his voice cannot be heard). The catcher, who is in a good position to see the play, can help when he sees a potential collision, by calling the name of the player who should catch the ball, for example, "Jane's catch!" (see Figure 4.15).

The proper catch is with both hands above the face, with the bare hand ready to clamp over the ball as soon as it hits the glove.

A fungo bat is good for a coach to use in hitting pop-ups. If he has trouble hitting pop-ups consistently, he can just throw the ball up. Figure 4.16 shows a coach using a tennis racket and ball with rookies, who may be scared of catching a hard ball in the beginning practices. We have seen enough rookies get hit on the head

4.13 On borderline plays between the second baseman and the shortstop, the shortstop should make the catch.

4.14 The center fielder moves into position to back up the shortstop, who is making the catch.

with a baseball because they misjudged it to know that Mike's technique with the tennis racket makes sense. Once they have mastered the technique of going to the ball, getting under it, and catching it directly overhead, they can be weaned from the tennis ball to the baseball.

Fly-Ball Drills

Coaches who just hit fly balls to a disorganized group of players in

4.15 The catcher gets rid of his mask and signals a pop-up, calling to the infielder who should catch it.

the outfield are giving practice only to the more aggressive players while risking injury at the same time. Not only can players be hit in the scramble to catch the fly ball, but if they have to throw the ball many times from the outfield back to the hitter, they are putting a strain on their throwing arm.

That kind of drill also fails to take advantage of the opportunity to coach an outfielder in another important job: making an accurate throw to the relay player.

We recommend an outfield drill involving three to five players and a coach. In a three-player drill, one is the outfielder, one is the relay, and one is the catcher. You can expand it to four or five players by adding one or two outfielders. Figure 4.17 shows the drill with three players and a coach. The coach hits fly balls to the outfielder, varying position and distance. The outfielder throws the ball to the glove side of the relay, and the relay pivots and throws to the

4.16 The coach uses a tennis racket and balls to teach rookie outfielders how to catch fly balls.

catcher. To add some competition and fun to the drill, we tell the kids to score two points for a catch, one point for a good throw to the relay, and one point for a good throw from the relay to the catcher. Each team of three keeps their point total and compares it with other teams of three.

When you expand the drill to include three outfielders, it is important to coach the importance of backing up one another, so that a ball that gets through one can be quickly retrieved by his backup outfielder.

Ground balls should also be hit to outfielders, and they should be taught how to block the ball by dropping to one knee and keeping the body in front of the ball. How many times have you seen a routine single turn into a triple or inside-the-park home run because the outfielder let the ball get through and roll to the fence?

4.17 Outfielder drill: The coach uses three players to teach catching fly balls and throwing to the relay, who throws to the catcher. Players rotate positions.

Situation Drills

After the basics have been taught, and your kids have been pegged for certain positions, you should go through team situation drills, such as one out, runner on third, fly to left field. We conduct them using runners to add realism to the drill. In the preceding example, we would have a runner on third base tag up after the catch and break for home. It would test the left fielder's throwing ability and accuracy, the catcher's catching and tagging ability, and the runner's speed and sliding ability.

The kids enjoy this kind of situation drill using runners, because it duplicates real game situations.

Make out a list of all of the various situations and use it in the drill. If you are rained out of a practice, then have a "skull session," using the same list and asking the specific players involved in a particular situation to tell you what they would do.

One of the most popular situation drills that your kids will enjoy practicing is the "hot-box" drill. Since it is a running as well as a fielding drill, we will cover it in the next chapter with the drills for running the bases.

5

DRILLS FOR BASERUNNING PRACTICE

Is running so basic that you don't have to teach it? You would think so until you meet your first rookie who runs on her heels or flails her arms as she runs. The basic running form is to lean forward, head down, run on toes, pump arms, eyes straight ahead.

The preceding chapter mentions that we have periodic foot races among the players in early practice, usually by age level, but ultimately to find out who is the fastest team member.

Make the race course 60 feet, tell them it is the distance between home and first, and emphasize that it is like a track meet, with the finish line being first base. Then ask them if they have ever seen a track meet where the runners slowed up as they reached the finish line. Get them to picture in their minds the track star breaking the finish line at full speed, and tell them that's the way you want them to cross first base. Also ask them if they have ever seen a track star, while running, look at anything but the finish-line tape.

We emphasize these two things: (1) Hit first base at full speed; and (2) never take your eyes off first base. The reason for this emphasis is that the two major errors your players are likely to make are slowing up as they near first base and looking at the ball as they run up the line.

There is something in the mind of your average rookie that makes her instinctively slow down as she approaches first base, whereas she should run through it on the foul line side at full speed (see Figure 5.1). Make sure your players understand the rules regarding overrunning first base. What makes them slow down may be the mistaken fear that they can be tagged out if they go too far beyond first base. In any event, it is a common problem with Little Leaguers, and it needs to be dealt with early. If, after we have established the principle of running through first base, players slow down in practice sessions, we make them run laps to help them remember.

The other natural tendency is to look at the ball instead of first base as they are running up the line. This has a tendency to slow the runner. If they are looking at anything other than first base, it

5.1 The base runner runs through first base at full speed.

should be the base coach, who will be giving them the windmill sign to keep going if the ball has gone through the outfielder or has been thrown wild to first. Another reason for urging the runner to look only at the base is to avoid injury. Often a first baseman will be forced to crowd the base to take a bad throw (see Figure 5.2), and the base runner needs to touch the foul-line side of the bag to avoid a collision.

The fear of getting caught off base is so great in the minds of many rookies that it inhibits their ability to run the bases. They instinctively stop and hold when they reach a base. We emphasize just the opposite—that a base is something you should leave as soon after you touch it as possible. When you are on base, you leave it on every pitch (as it reaches the plate), and you return to it only if you have to.

5.2 The first baseman is crowding the base, but the base runner hits the foul-line side of first base without breaking stride.

Run-When-You-Walk Drill

We teach the Pete Rose way of getting a walk. Rose was famous for running to first and taking a turn. In Little League it can mean an extra base if the other team is sleeping. If the catcher or pitcher is not watching the runner, or if the second baseman and short-stop are not covering second base, a savvy runner can run to first, make a turn, and keep on running to second. We have done it many times, and it is worth drilling both as a practice drill and in situation play drills. (Remember to teach your team the proper defense in this situation.)

Sliding Drill

To avoid painful "brush burns" on players' thighs, the sliding drill should be done in a sliding pit (with sawdust) if you have one, on soft dirt (hose it down well and then loosen it with a rake), or on grass that has been hosed. These are the sliding pointers that should be stressed:

- Run close to the ground and slide without breaking stride.
- Slide feet first with the left foot raised off the ground slightly. The right leg should be bent to assist in standing up quickly in case the ball is overthrown. (The head first slide is not for Little League.) Since metal spikes are not allowed, the raised foot will not hurt the baseman, but may knock the ball out of his glove.
- Slide on the right hip (body turned away from the throw), hands outstretched for balance.
- Aim for the center of the base.
- Relax your legs.
- Keep your hands off the ground.
- Be ready to scramble to your feet and keep going if the ball goes through.

- If you are safe and the baseman has the ball, call "time" immediately.
- Don't assume you are out if you hear a call or saw an out sign from the umpire. Infielders have been known to make the call, and umpires have been known to change their call if they see the tag out and then see the infielder drop the ball.
- Don't leave the base until you have seen the baseman get rid of the ball, and don't be fooled by a fake throw.

Stealing-Second Drill

Most stealing in Little League is on a passed ball or wild pitch. And with some teams, that is the only stealing that is done.

We coach the runner on first to go off two steps on every pitch as it crosses the plate (see Figure 5.3) and to go off as if she will

5.3 The runner on first is ready to push off as soon as the pitch crosses the plate.

keep going. If she does that, then she can keep going at full speed if the ball is hit, is pitched wild, or is passed by the catcher.

Attempt a steal early in the game to test the catcher. Do not attempt this with every player, only with the fast ones. Determine which players are your fastest through the foot-race drills.

The base-stealing drill is best done when the ground is soft, because the base runners are naturally expected to slide. It should involve the pitcher, catcher, pretend batter, runner, second baseman, and shortstop. The pitch is made, the catcher throws (with mask on), the runner breaks and slides, and the shortstop or second baseman makes the tag, with the other backing him (see Figure 5.4). In higher levels of baseball, the second baseman takes the throw with a right-handed batter up, and the shortstop with a left-handed batter. In Little League, we recommend that the manager designate who should take the throw and have him take it in every situation.

5.4 The second baseman has position but doesn't have the ball on a steal.

Stealing-Third Drill

We don't recommend having a runner steal third, unless on a wild pitch or passed ball, and then only when the ball is well out of reach of the catcher. The distance of 60 feet is just too short a throw from catcher to third baseman for the base runner to be able to beat. I might risk it if I see that a rookie third baseman or catcher has been inserted in the lineup; but it's too rare a play to merit drilling.

Stealing-Home Drill

Stealing home is an important play to drill, both offensively and defensively. Offensively, the base runner should be coached to go off the base as soon as the pitch reaches the plate, and keep on going on a wild pitch or passed ball. It is important that she (and the coach) observe

- The position of the third baseman
- The action of the catcher in returning the pitch to the pitcher
- Whether the pitcher covers home on a wild pitch or a passed ball

If the third baseman plays well off the base, with a runner on third, the runner can go down the line on every pitch as far as the third baseman is playing off the base. If the third baseman is well off the base and the catcher makes no attempt to force the runner back to third, the runner can break for home from her position down the line, as soon as the catcher releases the ball back to the pitcher. While the runner is running and sliding into home, the pitcher has to catch the ball and throw it back to the catcher, and the catcher has to make the tag. In most cases, it is no contest, with the runner scoring. (This is also known as a delayed steal and can be used at any base.)

In a game last season, we had the winning run on third base, bottom of the sixth with two outs and a weak hitter at bat. We signaled to the base runner on third to take a chance. She started down the line on the next pitch, and the catcher started up the line to meet her. When the catcher forced our runner back to third, she was two-thirds of the way up the line to third base, and no one was covering home. As soon as the catcher released the ball to the pitcher, on the mound, our runner broke for home, scored standing up, and the ball game was won! Obviously, the pitcher was in error for not covering home plate when the catcher started up the line toward third base. The pitcher is vulnerable in this situation, torn between leaving the mound and covering home. The runner should take advantage of the situation and do everything possible to steal home.

We have a drill we call "zebra," for lack of a better name. It is for a situation with a runner on third, two out, and a weak hitter at bat. The base runner deliberately breaks for home on the next pitch, forcing a rundown. We gamble on her scoring by outwitting the catcher and third baseman in the rundown, since the chances are the weak hitter would not have scored her anyway. Our record on scoring in the zebra situation was two out of three times, which made it worth the gamble.

Another situation that should be coached is watching what the catcher does when she has to go back to the screen to retrieve a passed ball or wild pitch. She may recover it too soon, and the pitcher covers home too quickly, to risk a steal. However, when the catcher sees that the runner on third is not breaking for home but holds on to the ball at the screen until the pitcher retreats to the mound and then releases it, the base runner can steal at the moment of release, because the catcher, wearing all of that equipment, has to throw the ball, run back to the plate, catch the ball, and make the tag.

"Hot-Box" Drill

The hot-box drill is probably the most popular; the kids even like to practice it on their own. At the Little League Baseball Camp at Williamsport we saw a hot-box game going on outside nearly every cabin during free time!

The hot-box drill the kids play on their own is usually a three-player drill, with one being the runner and the other two the infielders. However, the hot-box drill we recommend in practice is a five-player drill, with each infielder having a backup who rotates into the play whenever the fielder he backs up throws the ball. Figures 5.5, 5.6, and 5.7 explain three versions of this drill.

Figure 5.8 shows a hot-box situation between first and second bases, Figure 5.9 the play between second and third, and Figure 5.10 the play between third and home. In each case, as the fielder throws the ball, she moves away from the line of fire and falls in behind her former backup, who is now on the line of fire. This routine requires drilling until the fielders are able to do it smoothly and automatically. Teach your players to communicate so they know who is covering the different positions.

Defensively, the emphasis needs to be placed on four objectives:

- Make as few throws as possible.
- Chase the runner back to the previous base.
- Fake throws to force change in direction.
- Run her down if you can (as opposed to a throw that may go astray).

Offensively, the emphasis should be on the following:

- Force as many throws as possible.
- Fake direction change to force a throw.

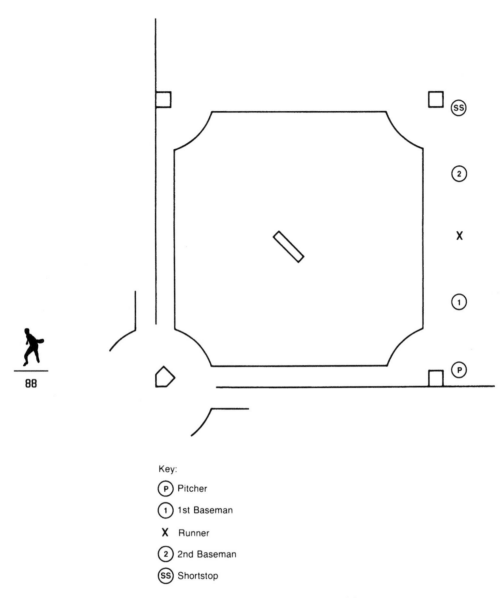

Key:

(P) Pitcher

(1) 1st Baseman

X Runner

(2) 2nd Baseman

(SS) Shortstop

5.5 "Hot box" drill between first and second base

- Try to get to the next base.
- Avoid the tag.

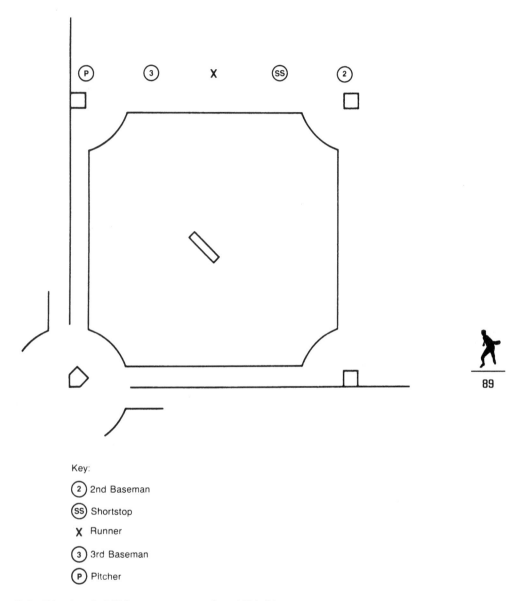

Key:

(2) 2nd Baseman

(SS) Shortstop

X Runner

(3) 3rd Baseman

(P) Pitcher

5.6 "Hot box" drill between second and third base

Notice in Figures 5.8 through 5.10 that the pitcher is involved in every rundown play. The importance of the pitcher as a contributing infielder cannot be better emphasized than in a hot-box drill.

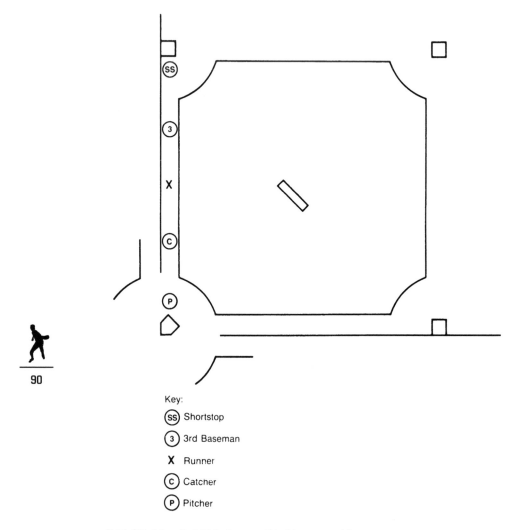

90

Key:

(ss) Shortstop

(3) 3rd Baseman

X Runner

(c) Catcher

(p) Pitcher

5.7 "Hot box" drill between third base and home

Base-Runner Signs

The three basic signs for a base coach are:

- Windmill: keep going
- Palms facing runner: stop
- Palms on ground: slide

5.8 The runner is trapped in the hot box between first and second. The pitcher, first baseman, second baseman, and shortstop are involved.

The best drill for base coaches and runners is for the coach to stand behind the third-base player as runners come around second, heading for third. In a stage whisper, tell the base coach either "Stop," "Slide," or "Keep going," and see if the coach gives the correct sign and if the base runner executes correctly.

Players enjoy being base coaches (see Figure 5.11), and we try to let the players who play the least coach the most as compensation. You can always call time and substitute a coach if you want to send special instructions to the base runner with a more savvy coach.

The base coaches need to be drilled on what they need to tell the base runner between pitches:

1. How many outs (index finger, one out; index finger and little finger, two outs)
2. Whether there are other runners on base

5.9 A hot box situation between second and third involves the second baseman, shortstop, third baseman, and pitcher.

5.10 The pitcher, catcher, third baseman, and shortstop try to tag out the runner in the hot box between third and home.

3. Applicable rules, such as run on anything or run on a ground ball. The coach should be picking these up from the dugout and repeating them to the base runner.

4. Run on a 3-2 count when there are two outs.

Situation Drills

In situation drills for base running, the coach stands near the pitcher's mound and all the players line up behind first base to take a turn as the coach calls out the situation. For a quicker workout, have all the players line up along the first-base line, draw a line in the dirt through second base, and have them run from their spot on the first base line to the same spot on the second base line. This drill can also be done for running from second to third and third to home.

Here is the list of the situations the coach will call out (left column) and what the runner is expected to do (right column):

5.11 Little League rules require that one base coach be a player, and we try to keep the coaching signs simple. This 10-year-old base coach's "hands on hip, finger in your ear, and spit" sign was totally ad-libbed.

93

From First Base

1. "The pitch reaches the front of the plate."

2. "It's a ground ball."

3. "The catcher missed the ball."

4. "It's a pop-up to the infield.

5. "The infielder misses the pop-up."

6. "It's a fly ball to the outfield."

---

1. Run three steps toward second.

2. Keep running to second.

3. Keep running to second.

4. Stop after three steps and watch to see if it is caught.

5. Run to second.

6. Go halfway to second and watch the outfielders.

7. "The outfielder catches it."	7. Return to first base.
8. "The outfielder misses it."	8. Run to second.
9. "There are runners on first and second with no outs (or one out); it's a pop-up to the infield."	9. Stay on the base (it's an infield fly).
10. "It's through the infield."	10. Think about going two bases.

From Second Base with Runner at First

Situations 1–10 are the same as running from first.

From Second Base with No Other Runners on Base

All situations except 2 and 5 are the same as running from first.

2. "It's a ground ball."	2. On a ground ball, the runner runs the three steps and stops. If the throw is to second or third, she gets back; if the throw is to first, she runs to third.
5. "The infielder misses the pop-up."	5. If the infielder misses the ball, she doesn't have to run.

From Third Base with Bases Loaded

All situations except 3 and 6 are the same as running from first. Situations 7, 8, and 10 are not applicable.

3. "The catcher missed the ball."	3. If the catcher misses the ball or if it's a wild pitch, the runner will go if it is easy to steal home or the game is tied in the last inning. (With a good catcher, the ball will have to bounce away from the catcher for there to be a good chance to steal.)
6. "It's a fly ball to the outfield."	6. On a fly ball to the outfield, the runner returns to the bag to tag up and score on a fly ball. She leaves the base as soon as the ball hits the outfielder's glove.

From Third Base Late in the Game with the Score Tied

1. "The pitch reaches the front of the plate."

    1. The best runners can take five steps.

2. "It's a ground ball."

    2. Only the fastest runner can score if the infielder throws to first.

3. "The catcher missed the ball."

    3. If it is hard to steal home, the runner goes only if the ball bounces to the left or right; fast runner takes a chance.

4. "It's a pop-up to the infield."

    4. Don't run.

5. "The infielder misses the pop-up."

    5. Don't run.

6. "It's a fly ball to the outfield."

    6. Tag up.

7. "The outfielder catches it."

    7. Run home after tagging.

8. "The outfielder misses it."

    8. Run home after tagging.

DRILLS FOR PREGAME PRACTICE

Pregame conditioning is important, but it is also important to condition the kids and their parents to understand that the players are expected to arrive at the field at least one half hour before game time and to spend that time in pregame conditioning, not in visiting the concession stand. Parents should avoid visiting the dugout so the players can concentrate on the game.

Pregame Routine

As players arrive at the field, have each grab a ball and begin to loosen up in either right or left field, depending on which dugout the team has for that game. One player should line up on the foul line and the other 10 yards into the outfield. After a few minutes of throwing warm-ups, the players should spread out to 15 yards apart and begin playing "Ten Points."

Ten Points is a game to break the monotony of throwing a ball back and forth. Many times good players get bored with throwing warm-ups and start throwing pop-ups or grounders or just lobbing the ball back and forth. They should understand the importance of warming up their arms and the discipline of doing it properly. In this game, a player gets one point for each throw that the other player catches directly in front of his chest, and two points for each ball that is caught directly in front of the face. The first to earn ten points wins.

If your facility has batting cages, work with a few players at a time throwing batting practice. Focus on the players who need it most, but don't forget to include your better players. If you do not have batting cages, throw some soft tosses just to loosen up.

About 20 minutes before game time, gather all of your players in a neatly organized group and begin working through an exercise regimen (see Figures 6.1 and 6.2). Emphasize stretching and coordination skills such as jumping jacks. After stretching, have them run from their location to the nearest foul pole, along the outfield fence to the other foul pole, and then back. They should stay together as a group to emphasize the team mentality.

6.1 Arm stretches help loosen the arms and back.

As soon as your starting battery arrives, have them warm up together with the team and then have them begin a pregame pitching warm-up. The pitcher and catcher should work the same distance apart as when they are on the field, and the pitcher should use a full windup but throw at three-quarter speed.

If your team is up for fielding practice, begin with that; if the opposing team is doing their infield practice, gather your team for a pregame pep talk and review of the signals, strategy, and game fundamentals. The more you review these fundamentals, the more your players will remember them.

When it is time to take fielding practice, have the players *run* onto the field and take their positions—including the pitcher and catcher. If you have substitutes, have them take the position they would most likely play during the game and alternate with the starting player. Work the infield first, then the outfield, and then the infield again. First get one out at first base, starting with grounders

6.2 Leg stretches help loosen legs and thighs.

to third, short, second, first, the pitcher and a bunt for the catcher. Next, do the "one and cover" exercise: a grounder to an infielder, who throws to first and then covers the bag for a throw from the catcher. If you have another coach, he can be hitting fly balls to the outfield from one of the foul lines beyond the basepaths, just to keep the players moving.

Outfield is next. Hit a fly ball to each of the outfielders and have them throw to their cutoff man at second base, third base, and home—in that order. Emphasize the cutoff man being in the correct position and the outfielder throwing accurately to the glove side of the cutoff man. If there is a second coach, the outfielders can continue getting fly balls as before, or they can *run* to the dugout and get ready for the game.

The infielders are now ready for their second drill. This should be turning the double play, throwing to home plate after charging a ground ball, and then following into home plate to receive a dribbler rolled by the catcher. The third baseman and first baseman should go to the dugout after their charge home, and the shortstop and second baseman should return to their positions for two "coming down" throws from the catcher after the pitcher simulates a pitch. There are many versions of this workout. We suggest you develop one like it but adjust the routine based on your team's skill level, personality, and field facilities.

The only way a player develops skills is to practice. Emphasize this to all players, and remind them of it constantly. We like to remind our players that they will play like they practice.

Figure 6.3 shows the positioning of coaches and players in this plan of pregame drills. Figure 6.4 diagrams what we call the around-the-horn throwing drill. It can be used as a pregame drill to loosen up the arms and fine-tune the accuracy of your infielders' throws. It can also be used in a regular practice drill by letting substitute fielders take a turn at each infield position, in rotation, as diagrammed.

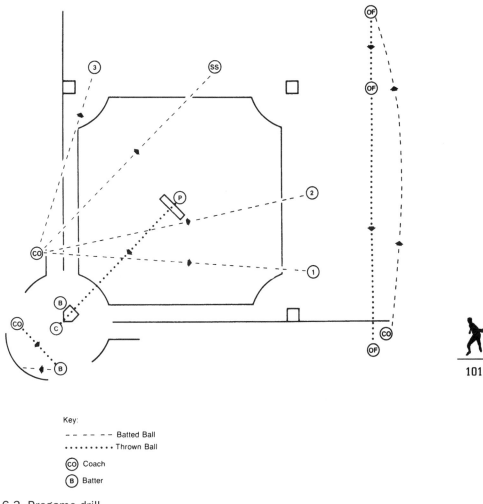

Key:

– – – – – – Batted Ball

• • • • • • • • Thrown Ball

(CO) Coach

(B) Batter

6.3 Pregame drill

Skull Drill

While the other team is warming up, get your team in the dugout for a pregame skull drill. Because of the short retention span of 9- to 12-year-olds, you can't review the basics too often. They should include the topics reviewed here.

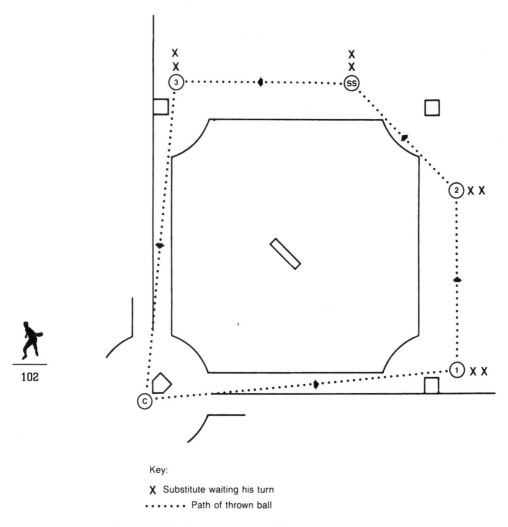

Key:

X Substitute waiting his turn

• • • • • • Path of thrown ball

6.4 Around-the-horn throwing drill

Batting Signals

Keep batting signals simple: hit (coach claps his hands); take (coach shows the bunting position, because he wants the batter to "fake bunt" to draw a ball from the pitcher); and bunt (coach touches his cap). To make the signs look complicated to confuse any would-be "sign stealers," tell your players that the real sign is the third one.

Normally, so the batter doesn't get confused, the first two signs are always the same, so he gets used to that sequence and is ready for the third sign. If the batter misses the sign, have him step out of the batter's box as a signal to the coach to repeat the sign.

Where to Stand in the Batter's Box

If the opposing pitcher has a strong fastball, remind the players to stand as far back in the batter's box as possible to give them maximum time to watch the pitch. Conversely, if he is a "junk pitcher," tell them to stand forward in the batter's box so they can hit the ball in front of the plate before it arches down.

Baserunning Signs

Baserunning signs also should be simple: slide (hands close to the ground); stop, standing up (hands at chest in stop signal); keep going (windmill with right arm). The most frequently forgotten base-coaching assignment is that of the on-deck batter, who should stand in a position where he can be seen by the runner coming from third to home.

Baserunning Rules

Review three basic rules of baserunning:

- With two outs, run on anything.
- With less than two outs, tag up on a fly ball.
- In a force-play situation, run on a ground ball.

Pitching/Catching Rules

Cover four rules for pitching and catching:

- Keep the ball low on the good hitters.
- Throw from the stretch position to the weak hitters if you are having control problems.

- The catcher must give the pitcher a good target, adjusting it to compensate. For example, give an inside target if the pitcher is consistently throwing outside.
- The pitcher must cover home with a runner on third in a wild pitch–passed ball situation.

We have a checklist of these coaching tips that I pull out of my pocket for the pregame skull session. The players expect it and can almost recite it. When they *can* recite it, I know they will have a good chance of remembering the coaching tips in game situations.

When working with children of Little League age, repetition is the only way you can hope to have them perform the way they should in a game situation. This means repetition in batting, fielding, baserunning, and pitching drills, and, also repetition in the important skull session part of baseball.

7

STRATEGY FOR WORKING WITH PARENTS

T he release of the first edition of *Managing Little League Baseball* by Ned McIntosh in 1985 prompted some media attention, since it was the first published book about Little League baseball. Favorable reviews appeared in *USA Today*, the Associated Press, and a number of city newspapers. Many of the reviews focused on the chapter titled "Parents and Pressure." Those two words were used together deliberately, because they represent the "cause and effect" of the ugly side of what is supposed to be a wholesome, fun experience for kids. The *Chicago Tribune*'s review said, "Little League, when used as the modifier for the word 'parent,' has become, in some circles, a synonym for abusive, overbearing, insensitive, or warped." Not only was this the first book published on Little League baseball, but it was released at a time when newspaper headlines were reporting many sad stories of "parent rage" and related problems inherent in youth sports. The ultimate example is the recent case of the hockey coach/father in Massachusetts who was murdered by another father during an argument after their sons' hockey game. Tragic and extreme, it nevertheless was a strange manifestation of the same kind of unreasonable, out-of-character anger that occurs in some Little League parents who see their children break into tears after striking out. Parental instinct takes over, and some parents look for someone to blame for making their child unhappy. Usually a coach or an umpire is the target.

As if that situation were not bad enough, *Sports Illustrated* published a special edition exposé in 1999 called "Do You Know Who Is Coaching Your Child?" It featured true stories of convicted child molesters who were coaching youth sports teams, underscoring the frightening fact that most youth sports organizations, in recruiting volunteers, make no effort to screen them. We need to make sure that we are providing positive role models for the children who are put into the hands of volunteers for a number of hours each week of each Little League season.

Fourteen years after *Managing Little League Baseball* was first published, a provocative book, *Why Johnny Hates Sports* was written by Fred Engh, president of NAYS (National Alliance of Youth Sports). Its subtitle is "Why Organized Youth Sports Are Failing Our Children and What We Can Do About It." The simple answer to Engh's question of why so many youngsters get turned off to sports is that many adults—parents and coaches—take the fun out of kids' sports. Engh's book exposed the ugly side of youth sports, but it proposed a solution to the complex problem of parents and coaches making youth sports unattractive to the children they presumably want to help. Engh does not recommend that parents pull their children out of youth sports. He does tell them to take the pressure off their children and bring pressure to bear on the sports organizations.

In his book Engh quotes a comprehensive study of youth sports conducted by the Youth Sports Institute at Michigan State University that lists the top 10 reasons why boys and girls drop out of youth sports. Among the major reasons for both sexes were: "It was no longer fun," "There was too much pressure," and "The coach was a poor teacher."

The remedial program NAYS initiated calls for parent education, mandatory coach's training and certification, and careful screening of prospective coaches, including criminal background checks, just as schools do when they recruit teachers. NAYS proposes raising an organization's registration fee by one dollar to cover the cost of fingerprinting and background screening.

The place to start screening Little League coaches is Tee Ball, where many managers are first appointed. From that point on, coaching often becomes addictive; a parent who volunteers to manage his child's Tee Ball team will often follow that child as his manager to each successively higher level. *The Little League Guide to Tee Ball* includes a chapter on parent and parent/coach objectivity; lack of such objectivity is the cause of much of the unseemly behavior of adults involved in youth sports programs. The chapter includes a 50-item true/false test of parent/coach objectivity/ subjectivity. A typical entry is: "If I am a manager putting in a lot of volunteer hours, I would be justified in playing my child more than the other players on the team." Test scores that indicate a high level of subjectivity should raise a red flag about a managerial candidate.

The NAYS program includes codes of ethics that both parents and coaches must sign at the beginning of each sport season. If parents and coaches work together to uphold these codes, the result will be less pressure on the children and a safer and more positive experience for all involved.

We must be conscious that a new generation of parents is moving up to Little League each year, while the more seasoned parents have moved on. Unless good attitudes and parent control have been established in your lower-level leagues, that influx of one-third new parents could be enough to upset the stability of last year's good crop of parents. As mentioned earlier, the younger the player, the more protective the parents are, and the more likely to overreact when their child is called out on strikes, is criticized by the coach, or breaks into tears for any number of reasons that are dictated by the pressure of his first serious encounter with competitive sports. And as recommended in *Managing Little League Baseball*, the more communication a manager establishes with his team's parents, the less likely it is that there will be misunderstandings and confrontations between parents and the coach.

PARENTS' CODE OF ETHICS

- I will encourage good sportsmanship by demonstrating positive support for all players, coaches, and officials at every game, practice, or other youth sports event.
- I will place the emotional and physical well-being of my child ahead of a personal desire to win.
- I will insist that my child play in a safe and healthy environment.
- I will support coaches and officials working with my child, in order to encourage a positive and enjoyable experience for all.
- I will demand a sports environment for my child that is free of drugs, tobacco, and alcohol, and will refrain from their use at all youth sports events.
- I will remember that the game is for youth—not for adults.
- I will do my very best to make youth sports fun for my child.
- I will ask my child to treat other players, coaches, fans, and officials with respect, regardless of race, sex, creed, or ability.
- I promise to help my child enjoy the youth sports experience by doing whatever I can, such as being a respectful fan, assisting with coaching, or providing transportation.
- I will require that my child's coach be trained in the responsibilities of being a youth sports coach, and the coach upholds the Coaches' Code of Ethics.

© National Alliance for Youth Sports

Mike Powers agrees about the need for communication between managers/coaches and parents. Figure 7.1 is a copy of the letter and team roster that he sends to the parents of his players. Note that in the third paragraph he says to the parents ". . . and I will leave it to you to develop the parent organization that St. Matthews Little League expects us to have." So many managers think that they have to carry the whole burden of the team. Mike makes it clear that he expects the parents to assume part of the responsibility. It then becomes an adult team effort running parallel with their children's team effort on the field.

In Mike's league in St. Matthews, Kentucky, the Board of Directors sends a questionnaire to all parents, asking them to evaluate the league and give their recommendations (see Figure 7.2). It even asks parents to evaluate their child's manager and coach. The questions demonstrate the league's goals of sportsmanship, skills, enthusiasm, and so forth. The absence of emphasis on won-lost record puts that in its proper perspective.

If you build it, the parents will come. Communicate with them.

COACHES' CODE OF ETHICS

- I will place the emotional and physical well-being of my players ahead of a personal desire to win.
- I will treat each player as an individual, remembering the large range of emotional and physical development for the same age group.
- I will do my best to provide a safe playing situation for my players.
- I will promise to review and practice the basic first aid principles needed to treat injuries of players.
- I will do my best to organize practices that are fun and challenging for all my players.
- I will lead by example in demonstrating fair play and sportsmanship to all my players.
- I will be knowledgeable in the rules of each sport that I coach and I will teach these rules to my players.
- I will use those coaching techniques appropriate for each of the skills that I teach.
- I will remember that I am a youth sports coach and that the game is for children and not adults.

© National Alliance for Youth Sports

In summary, the two keys to dealing with parents are organization and communication.

Organization

The local league board should anticipate the reasons for parental problems and establish an organization that will handle them equitably. The board itself should consist of enough *nonparticipating* members—that is, members who are not managers or coaches—to remove bias, and the appearance of bias, from board decisions. If a board member is a manager, coach, or parent of a player whose team is involved in a dispute, that member should be excused from participating in, or voting on, the dispute.

Potential disputes over umpiring should be anticipated by following the suggestions in this book for recruiting, training, and assigning umpires, so that in no case will an umpire related to any player or coach of a team be assigned to handle a game that team plays. Potential disputes over rules should be avoided by following the suggestions for holding mandatory training meetings of managers, coaches, and umpires—that they attend together—so they all will be "reading from the same page" with respect to the rules.

Communication

111

Managers should be urged to have meetings and communications with the parents of their players before the season begins to explain what parents should expect from the manager and coaches and, in turn, what they should expect from the parents. The volunteer opportunities for parents should be explained, and parents should be encouraged to do their part. They should be encouraged to support their team but not criticize the opposing team or the umpires. Managers should make it clear that they are responsible for the conduct of the spectators and that an unruly parent can be ordered off the premises by the umpire or risk forfeiting the game for the manager's team.

The board should be encouraged to establish both internal and external communications vehicles to keep everyone informed—for example, a newsletter, bulletin board, press releases, and so on—to provide both information and recognition.

FIRST NATIONAL BANK TEAM

March 24, 2003

Dear First National Parents,

Jon and I are very pleased to have your children on the team. We will try our best to do all the right things for the team and your children. We will teach them good sportsmanship, how to work together as a team, and how to work to improve. We will also be as objective as we can in determining who will play each position and where they will bat in the batting order.

Practices will be held at St. Albert's field at 5:45 P.M. Monday through Thursday for the first two weeks (March 24–April 3), with a scrimmage game being planned for Saturday, March 29. Then we will *not* have practice during the school spring break, but will resume on Monday, April 14, at 5:45 P.M., and practice Monday through Thursday of that week. If it rains during practices, we'll move to my garage for a skull session (1810 Girard). The first game and the parade will be on April 19.

On April 3, we will have a parents' meeting at the field after practice to assure that we have volunteers for all the parent positions: business manager, player agent, picnic chairman, etc. We have all been through this several times before, and I will leave it to you to develop the parent organization that St. Matthews Little League expects us to have. (I will have descriptions for each of these parent positions with me at practice if you would like copies.)

Also, if anyone who has a camcorder would be willing to film some during practices or games, please talk with us.

If you have any questions or suggestions, let us know.

Sincerely,

Mike Powers
Manager

Jon Mindrum
Coach

Figure 7.1 Letter to parents and team roster

2003 Roster   St. Matthews Little League Baseball, Inc.   **Team Name: First National**

PLAYERS	AGE	BIRTHDATE	JERSEY NO.	PARENTS	ADDRESS	ZIP	PHONE
Michael Bailey	11	10/1/91		Ron/Sharon	212 Blankenbaker	40207	555-5000
Brian Clarke	12	4/1/91		Lloyd/Janet	224 Bramton Rd.	40207	555-0494
Scott Herman	12	10/25/90		Jan	1303 Ambridge Dr.	40207	555-6072
Jason Hawkins	12	1/16/91		Dennis/Sheryl	180 Vernon	40206	555-6340
Grayson Abell	11	6/24/92		Darnell	1010 Ambridge Dr.	40207	555-4655
Michael Mindrum	11	12/2/91		Jon/Janet	2319 Stoneleigh Ct.	40222	555-6288
Tom Powers	11	4/18/92		Mike/Kathy	1810 Girard Dr.	40222	555-0497
Chad Guelda	11	12/4/91		Charles/Maryle	4734 Brownsboro Rd.	40207	555-5590
Scott Scholtz	10	8/13/92		Jan Reis/Dawn	6303 Glenn Hill Rd.	40222	555-8090
Doug Abell	10	10/8/92		Doug/Rose	1004 Weymouth Ct.	40222	555-0856
Sam Graham	10	10/31/92		Kyle/Kathy	4802 Bilander Rd.	40222	555-0383
Stephen Webb	11	2/2/92		Bob/Patricia	7800 Pine Meadows	40222	555-2660

Manager Mike Powers   Phone 555-0497   Days Mon.-Thurs.   Times 5:45 P.M.

Coach Jon Mindrum   Phone 555-6288   Locations St. Alberts

Business Mgr. _____ Phone _____   Parents Auxillary Rep. _____ Phone _____

Scorekeeper _____ Phone _____   Telephone Chrm. _____ Phone _____

Team Picnic Chrm. _____ Phone _____

Concession Stand Tele. _____

113

Dear Parents,

Your child's participation in St. Matthews Little League Baseball is intended to be a beneficial and positive experience. The objective is to provide a healthful activity while promoting an appreciation for good sportsmanship, teamwork, and discipline.

To assist us in assuring this goal is achieved, we would appreciate your thoughts, observations, and comments in completing the questionnaire on the reverse side. Hopefully, your input will enable us to maintain, or improve, the fine program we have at St. Matthews.

While we ask that you include your name, address, and phone number, it is not a requirement. Please return your completed questionnaire to the concession stand before you leave the park today.

Thank you for taking the time to assist us.

Board of Directors, St. Matthews Little League Baseball, Inc.

Figure 7.2 Parents' questionnaire and cover letter

ST MATTHEWS LITTLE LEAGUE BASEBALL PROGRAM EVALUATION QUESTIONNAIRE

Team _____

Please circle the number that expresses your impressions of the Little League program. Five (5) indicates strong agreement; three (3), neutral; one (1), strong disagreement. If you are in strong disagreement with any question, please provide us with your thoughts in the Comments section.

1. The program teaches the importance of good sportsmanship.   5 4 3 2 1

2. Your child enjoyed and looked forward to practice.   5 4 3 2 1

3. Your child enjoyed and looked forward to the games. 5 4 3 2 1

4. You feel your child improved his/her skills during the season.   5 4 3 2 1

5. How do you evaluate the program's equipment?   5 4 3 2 1

6. How do you evaluate the program's facilities?   5 4 3 2 1

7. Your child's manager/coach was enthusiastic/ positive during games and practices.   5 4 3 2 1

8. Please evaluate the manager's/coach's effectiveness during games and practices in regard to:

   Teaching skills   5 4 3 2 1

   Individual attention   5 4 3 2 1

   Gaining your child's attention   5 4 3 2 1

9. Please provide your overall rating of:
   The team manager   5 4 3 2 1

   The team coach   5 4 3 2 1

10. You are interested in your child participating in next year's baseball program.   5 4 3 2 1

11. The St. Matthews Little League program met your expectations.   5 4 3 2 1

12. Please rate the overall St. Matthews Little League program.   5 4 3 2 1

COMMENTS: Please provide us with your thoughts regarding any problems you feel exist or any suggestions you have.

_____

_____

_____

_____

_____

_____

_____

_____

_____

_____

_____

_____

If you are interested in participating in the operation of the St. Matthews Little League program, please indicate your area of interest:

☐ Team Manager* ☐ Team Coach* ☐ Scorekeeper*

☐ Umpire* ☐ Board Member*

*Indicate Major, Minor or Tee-Ball division

OPTIONAL:

Parent's Name (PLEASE PRINT) _____

Child's Name _____

Address _____

Phone _____

Team _____

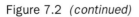

Figure 7.2 *(continued)*

8

STRATEGY FOR TRAINING UMPIRES, MANAGERS, AND COACHES

A recent conversation among a group of our managers touched on the caliber of the umpiring during the preceding week in our league. Each manager had a story about the one the umpires missed, and naturally the managers whose teams lost were the most critical of the umpiring.

To play the devil's advocate, we asked them if they had ever seen an umpire change a judgment call. They all admitted they had not, but in the discussion it became clear that not all of them really understood the difference between a judgment call and a rule call. For the reader who may also be unclear about the distinction, examples of judgment calls are:

- Balls and strikes
- Out or safe
- Leaving base too soon

Examples of rule calls are:

- Batting out of order
- Infield fly rule (although judgment can be a factor in determining position of ball and reasonable effort needed to catch it)
- Interference or obstruction

It is clear that judgment calls are more frequent, and even some rule calls are affected by judgment. And there is no doubt that most disputes are over the judgment calls of balls and strikes and decisions of out or safe at the bases (see Figure 8.1).

We then asked why they wasted the time, energy, and frustration over a judgment call when they all admitted they had never seen an umpire reverse himself on one. They were stuck for an answer

8.1 The umpire is in proper position to make his call at first base.

until one of them finally said, "To keep him honest." In a case where the umpire was obviously wrong and may let the next close one go your way, that may make some sense.

Effects of Calls

An umpire's alleged bad call will seldom *directly* affect the outcome of a game, but it is possible that it could *indirectly* affect it in several ways.

There are very few instances in which an umpire's judgment call directly affects the outcome of a game. Those few instances have been situations such as two outs, bottom of the sixth, and the tying run on third trying to score. The umpire must make a safe/out judgment call on a close play, and the manager whose team gets the wrong call will argue that the game was decided on the umpire's call, forgetting the many other crucial plays during the game that affected the outcome, in which the umpire may not have even been a factor.

More frequent are the cases in which an umpire's call has an *indirect* effect on a game. The most frequent cases have been those in which players allowed an umpire's call to affect them emotionally so badly that they could not perform well physically after the call. Such situations arise when pitchers blow up over an umpire's ball/strike call and completely lose their pitching effectiveness, or batters are so affected on a third-strike call that they are still thinking about it when they blow an easy ground ball in the defensive half of the inning. And on their next time at bat, they are still basket cases.

The high-strung, uptight Little Leaguer is most susceptible, and some players are either naturally that way or parent-pressured that way. They will lose their cool over an umpire's close call that doesn't go their way, which may not have *any* effect on the game, but because they lost their cool they are unable to regain it again throughout the rest of the game. Subconsciously it may even be an escape valve from the pressure—if they don't do well during the rest of the game, it was all the umpire's fault. That kind of pressure on their parents' part helps contribute to the parent problems covered in Chapter 7.

Invisible Umpires

What's the answer? We preach the philosophy that the umpires are invisible. They aren't even there; they are programmed robots that sometimes call them your way and sometimes the other way. They are lights on the scoreboard that tell you the balls and strikes and outs. Forget they exist!

Reinforce that philosophy every time a batter looks to the bench for sympathy on a called strike, comes back to the dugout after being called out on a close base play, or looks to the dugout from the pitcher's mound after a ball that she thought should have been called a strike. Just say, "The umpire's invisible!" and she will get the message.

As any coach will tell you, so much in sports is mental. A Little League coach must mentally as well as physically condition players how to play and how to accept disappointment as well as victory.

There is an old cliché, "The customer is always right," which is sometimes amended to "The customer is always right, even when he's wrong!" The analogy applies to umpires as well: The umpire is always right, *even when he's wrong*!

You need to press that point to your players by getting them to *believe* that umpires are invisible; that they call as many close ones for you as against you; that they just call 'em as they see 'em. To the players who persist in criticizing the umpire's calls, you may need to get even tougher and threaten to bench them.

Will umpires ever deliberately cheat? In my experience, the only umpires whose integrity could be questioned are those who are dragged out of the stands and asked to "volunteer." Invariably they are the fathers of the players on one competing team or the other. They may not know the rules, or if they do, they may have a bias when calling a close play. Since the perception of bias is there, spectators will assume it is in fact present.

Preseason Organizing

In *Managing Little League Baseball*, the importance of organizing preseason training meetings of managers, coaches, and umpires (in the same meetings) was stressed. We required every Major League and Minor League team to provide an umpire for the opposite league, and we then recruited other adults to fill out the assigned three-member crews. We also published a list of alternates and gave each umpire the responsibility of calling an alternate to take his place if he couldn't make an assignment. We do not pay our umpires, and we schedule them for only two evenings per week. That is certainly not asking too much of any umpire.

A number of our coaches and managers umpire in the opposite league, so it does require a scheduling job to make sure they are not assigned to umpire on a night when their team plays. We also have to schedule to make sure no dads will handle their kids' games.

One thing we have added to our training for umpires and coaches, since *Managing Little League Baseball* was published, is a "final exam," which we have reproduced at the end of this chapter. Anyone who scores 100 percent is well qualified to coach or umpire, with respect to understanding the basic rules. We have included an answer key to the exam and have noted the rule that applies to each question. If you are uncertain about an answer, a review of the appropriate rule will supply it. Please check, because there are several tricky questions.

Skull Sessions

You can't expect to have a good rapport between managers, coaches, and umpires unless you develop it. Just as we recommend skull sessions between coaches and players on your team, we also recommend periodic skull sessions between managers, coaches, and umpires in your league during the season.

Figure 8.2 is the training program outline for our initial training sessions with managers, coaches, and umpires. We augment it by having an experienced umpire teach umpire field positions. We have tried one, two, and three meetings and found that one is too few and three is too many. The Saturday before our season opens, we have a day of practice games, with every team playing and every umpire crew working. And just as managers are observing and coaching their players, we have umpire coaches observing and constructively coaching the umpires.

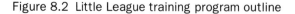

Little League Training Program Outline

A. GENERAL INFORMATION
   1. Ages of players
   2. Number of players per team
   3. Number of players per age level
   4. Dates of player drafts
   5. Dates of player cuts
   6. Roster deadlines
   7. Opening day
   8. Adding players to fill vacancies

Figure 8.2 Little League training program outline

B. LOCAL LEAGUE RULES
  1. Starting times of games
  2. Rainout schedule
  3. Substitutions (see Reg. IV [i], page 13; Rules 3.03, 3.05, 3.06, 3.07, and 3.08, page 29)
  4. Mercy rule
  5. Managers, Coaches, and Spectator Control (see Reg. XIV, page 16; rules 4.06 and 4.07, page 31)

C. KEY RESPONSIBILITIES OF UMPIRES
  1. Authority (Rule 9.01, page 47)
  2. Judgment call final (Rule 9.02 [a], page 47)
  3. Manager may appeal rule interpretation (Rule 9.02 [b] and [c], page 47)
  4. Conflicting decisions on same play by two umpires (Rule 9.04 [c], page 48)
  5. Deciding fitness of field (Rules 3.10 and 4.01 [d], page 30)
  6. Starting game (Rule 4.01, page 30)
  7. Called games and tie games (Rules 4. 10 and 4.11, page 32; Rule 4.12, page 33; examples on page 62)
  8. Forfeited games (Rules 4.15, 4.16, 4.17, and 4.18, page 33)
  9. Protested games (Rule 4.19, pages 33 and 34)
  10. Live and dead ball (Rule 5.02, page 34; Rules 5.08, 5.09, 5.10, 5.11, page 35)
  11. Umpires hand signs ("The Right Call," pages 5, 10, 22, 25, 31, 35, 37, 41, 43)
  12. Base umpires' field positions ("Umpire in Little League," pages 9–26)

D. KEY RULES REGARDING THE BATTER
  1. When pitcher ready (Rule 6.02 [b], page 36)
  2. Both feet in batter's box (Rule 6.03, page 36)
  3. Batter out (Rule 6.05, page 36; and Rule 6.06, page 37)
  4. Batting out of turn (Rule 6.07, pages 37 and 38)
  5. Hit by pitched ball (Rule 6.08 [b], page 38)
  6. Foul ball (Definition, page 25)
  7. Foul tip (Definition, page 26)
  8. Infield fly rule (Definition, page 26; Rule 7.08 [f], page 41; Rule 6.05 [e] and [1], page 36)
  9. Strike and strike zone (Definitions, page 27)
  10. Hitting pitch on the bounce (Definitions, "In flight," page 26)
  11. Intentional walk (Rule 4.03 [a], page 31)

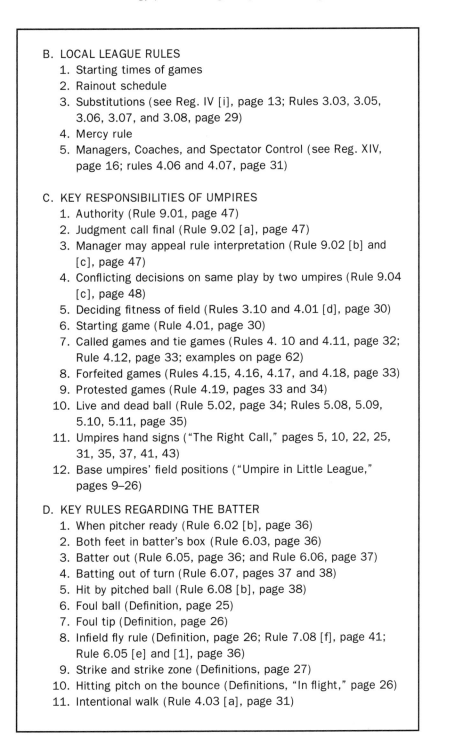

123

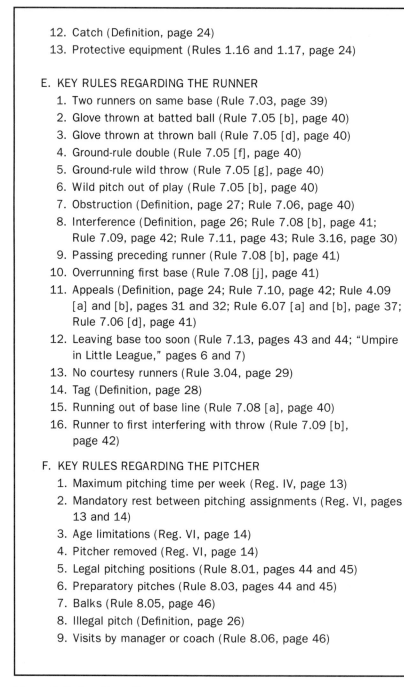

12. Catch (Definition, page 24)

13. Protective equipment (Rules 1.16 and 1.17, page 24)

E. KEY RULES REGARDING THE RUNNER

  1. Two runners on same base (Rule 7.03, page 39)

  2. Glove thrown at batted ball (Rule 7.05 [b], page 40)

  3. Glove thrown at thrown ball (Rule 7.05 [d], page 40)

  4. Ground-rule double (Rule 7.05 [f], page 40)

  5. Ground-rule wild throw (Rule 7.05 [g], page 40)

  6. Wild pitch out of play (Rule 7.05 [b], page 40)

  7. Obstruction (Definition, page 27; Rule 7.06, page 40)

  8. Interference (Definition, page 26; Rule 7.08 [b], page 41; Rule 7.09, page 42; Rule 7.11, page 43; Rule 3.16, page 30)

  9. Passing preceding runner (Rule 7.08 [b], page 41)

10. Overrunning first base (Rule 7.08 [j], page 41)

11. Appeals (Definition, page 24; Rule 7.10, page 42; Rule 4.09 [a] and [b], pages 31 and 32; Rule 6.07 [a] and [b], page 37; Rule 7.06 [d], page 41)

12. Leaving base too soon (Rule 7.13, pages 43 and 44; "Umpire in Little League," pages 6 and 7)

13. No courtesy runners (Rule 3.04, page 29)

14. Tag (Definition, page 28)

15. Running out of base line (Rule 7.08 [a], page 40)

16. Runner to first interfering with throw (Rule 7.09 [b], page 42)

F. KEY RULES REGARDING THE PITCHER

  1. Maximum pitching time per week (Reg. IV, page 13)

  2. Mandatory rest between pitching assignments (Reg. VI, pages 13 and 14)

  3. Age limitations (Reg. VI, page 14)

  4. Pitcher removed (Reg. VI, page 14)

  5. Legal pitching positions (Rule 8.01, pages 44 and 45)

  6. Preparatory pitches (Rule 8.03, pages 44 and 45)

  7. Balks (Rule 8.05, page 46)

  8. Illegal pitch (Definition, page 26)

  9. Visits by manager or coach (Rule 8.06, page 46)

124

Figure 8.2 *(continued)*

We assign three umpires to a crew and appoint crew chiefs from among our more experienced, more dependable umpires. We didn't used to do that, but we found that the title of crew chief gave that umpire an extra responsibility that she took to heart. Rarely did a crew chief not show up, and often she would get on members of her crew who were late or failed to get a substitute when unable to serve. It was not unusual to have only two out of three assigned umpires show; last-minute work or personal problems do occur. In such cases, two umpires can handle the game. We schedule three with the expectation that we will never have fewer than two. But it was extremely rare to have only one show, and we never had no members of an assigned crew show.

Attached as Figure 8.3 is our schedule for a recent season, listing all the names and phone numbers of team managers, umpires, and alternate umpires, in addition, of course, to the league schedule and umpiring assignments. Local rules were also attached in order to provide in one packet everything a manager, coach, or umpire needed for communications. We made enough copies available for every manager, coach, and umpire in the league, and put each individual's name on a set, so those who missed the meeting when they were passed out would be sure to get their set at the next opportunity. We had extra copies at the refreshment stand and posted the sheets, page by page, on our bulletin board.

Naturally, rule books were also provided to every manager, coach, and umpire, and extra copies were kept on hand. We provided umpires with uniforms—cap, shirt, and jacket—and insisted they wear them to add professionalism to their appearance. We provided each umpire a counter and had extra counters present. In the first training meeting, we asked all experienced umpires to search their jackets and drawers at home and bring in all of their excess counters. You would be surprised what a collection some had accumulated!

TO: Little League umpires and managers

FROM: Umpire-in-Chief

RE: Umpiring schedule and procedures

Attached are the team and umpiring schedules for this season. Please mark your calendar for the days you play and/or umpire. Note the following procedures:

1. *Schedule conflicts.* We have avoided all conflicts with the game schedules of those umpires who coach or play for another team. If you find you have a personal conflict with any assigned dates, please take the responsibility of obtaining your own replacement. Trade dates with another umpire, call one of the umpires on alternate list (all umpires' names and phone numbers are attached), call your crew chief, or call me; but don't just fail to show, since you may cause the delay or postponement of a game.

2. *Equipment.* Please wear dark trousers to complete your uniforms, and always be in complete uniform to add professionalism to your position. Game balls should be obtained at the concession stand, and equipment is in the scorekeeper's room. Please return all equipment after the game.

3. *Postponed games.* It is the responsibility of the home team manager to notify the umpires if a game will be postponed for any reason. Otherwise, teams and umpires should report to the field and the question of whether a game should start or not will be decided in accordance with the rules. *Please decide then, with teams and umpires present, when the game will be rescheduled.* (See chart indicating when game should be rescheduled in the attached local rules.)

   Umpires who have a schedule conflict with the rescheduled date should take the responsibility of getting a replacement, but if managers make last-minute schedule changes, then the home team manager must be responsible for obtaining the umpires.

   Names and phone numbers of umpires, alternate umpires, and home team managers are attached for your use in communicating with each other.

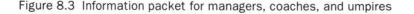

Figure 8.3 Information packet for managers, coaches, and umpires

Thanks for your cooperation and service to our youngsters. If you have any questions, feel free to call me at home (555-4651) or at work (555-3000).

Major League

TEAM	MANAGERS	PHONE
Pirates	Brooks Groves	555-3230
Yankees	Bill Cook	555-4356
Giants	Ned McIntosh	555-4651
Reds	Sonny Talbert	555-3041
A's (Birch River)	Bobby Mullens	555-4641
Cardinals	Jim Fitzwater	555-2292
Padres	Dave Keenan	555-5257
Phillies	Cotton Snuffer	555-1079
Expos	Delmar Tate	555-1225
Cubs	Dave Whitlock	555-2886

Umpire Crews

CREW A		CREW D	
John D. McClung*	555-1248	Buell Moses*	555-4393
Jeff Girod	555-3422	Lee Tate	555-1225
T. Tom Cook	555-3137	Bobby White	555-3399

CREW B		CREW E	
Bob Hennessey*	555-6466	Steve Ramsey*	555-2257
Arthur Corbett	555-4938	Dennis Childress	555-4736
Sam Argento	555-4540	Mike Burke	555-5823

CREW C

		ALTERNATES	
Joe Whitlock*	555-4107	Stan Smith	555-3472
Stan Smith	555-3472	Dennis Childress	555-4736
Bob Hughes	555-2041	Floyd Friend	555-5390
		Tom McGirl	555-6419

*Crew Chief—responsible for assigning umpire positions.

Major League Schedule

TEAM NUMBERS

1	Yankees	6	Padres
2	Reds	7	Phillies
3	Pirates	8	Cubs
4	Giants	9	Cards
5	A's	10	Expos

PRACTICE SATURDAY, APRIL 12

10:00 A.M.	2	vs.	6	Umpire Crew A
12:00 noon	1		7	Umpire Crew C
2:00 P.M.	5		8	Umpire Crew E
4:00 P.M.	3		9	Umpire Crew D
6:00 P.M.	4		10	Umpire Crew B

(first team listed is home team)

OPENING DAY, SATURDAY, APRIL 19 (RAIN DATE: 4/26)

10:30 A.M.	1	vs.	6	Umpire Crew B
12:30 P.M.	2		7	Umpire Crew D
2:00 P.M.	3		8	Umpire Crew A
3:30 P.M.	4		9	Umpire Crew C
5:00 P.M.	5		10	Umpire Crew E

128

Figure 8.3 (continued)

First Half

DAY	DATE	TIME	H	V	UMPIRE CREW
M	4/21	5:30	1	3	A
		7:30	2	4	A
T	4/22	5:30	5	7	B
		7:30	6	8	B
W	4/23	5:30	10	2	D
		7:30	9	1	D
Th	4/24	5:30	4	6	C
		7:30	3	5	C
F	4/25	5:30	7	9	E
		7:30	8	10	E
M	4/28	5:30	1	4	C
		7:30	5	8	C
T	4/29	5:30	3	6	B
		7:30	7	10	B
W	4/30	5:30	8	1	A
		7:30	9	2	A
Th	5/1	5:30	10	3	E
		7:30	4	7	E
F	5/2	5:30	2	5	D
		7:30	6	9	D

DAY	DATE	TIME	H	V	UMPIRE CREW
M	5/5	5:30	1	5	B
		7:30	2	6	B
T	5/6	5:30	3	7	A
		7:30	4	8	A
W	5/7	5:30	6	10	D
		7:30	5	9	D
Th	5/8	5:30	8	2	C
		7:30	7	1	C
F	5/9	5:30	10	4	E
		7:30	9	3	E
M	5/12	5:30	3	4	D
		7:30	1	2	D
T	5/13	5:30	5	6	B
		7:30	9	10	B
W	5/14	5:30	7	8	A
		7:30	2	3	A
Th	5/15	5:30	10	1	E
		7:30	4	5	E
F	5/16	5:30	8	9	C
		7:30	6	7	C

Second Half

DAY	DATE	TIME	H	V	UMPIRE CREW
M	5/19	5:30	3	1	D
		7:30	4	2	D
T	5/20	5:30	8	6	A
		7:30	7	5	A
W	5/21	5:30	2	10	B
		7:30	1	9	B
Th	5/22	5:30	6	4	C
		7:30	5	3	C
F	5/23	5:30	10	8	E
		7:30	9	7	E
M	5/26	5:30	8	5	A
		7:30	4	1	A
T	5/27	5:30	6	3	B
		7:30	10	7	B
W	5/28	5:30	2	9	E
		7:30	1	8	E
Th	5/29	5:30	7	4	D
		7:30	3	10	D
F	5/30	5:30	5	2	C
		7:30	9	6	C

DAY	DATE	TIME	H	V	UMPIRE CREW
M	6/2	5:30	6	2	B
		7:30	5	1	B
T	6/3	5:30	7	3	C
		7:30	8	4	C
W	6/4	5:30	9	5	A
		7:30	10	6	A
Th	6/5	5:30	2	8	E
		7:30	1	7	E
F	6/6	5:30	3	9	D
		7:30	4	10	D
M	6/9	5:30	2	1	A
		7:30	4	3	A
T	6/10	5:30	6	5	D
		7:30	8	7	D
W	6/11	5:30	10	9	C
		7:30	3	2	C
Th	6/12	5:30	5	4	B
		7:30	7	6	B
F	6/13	5:30	9	8	E
		7:30	1	10	E
M	6/16	5:30	7	2	A
		7:30	6	1	A
T	6/17	5:30	9	4	B
		7:30	8	3	B
W	6/18	5:30	10	5	C

Figure 8.3 *(continued)*

LOCAL MAJOR LEAGUE RULES

1. First game starts at 5:30 P.M. No new inning should start after 7:15 P.M. (Exception: A tie game should be allowed to continue until finished.)

2. Second game starts at 7:30 P.M. No new inning should start after 9:30 P.M. (Exception: On Fridays and Saturdays and after school is out.)

3. Rainouts must be played as follows:

   First rainout of week: Saturday, 10:00 A.M.
   Second rainout of week: Saturday, 12:00 noon
   Third rainout of week: Saturday, 1:30 P.M.
   Fourth rainout of week: Saturday, 3:00 P.M.
   Fifth rainout of week: Saturday, 4:30 P.M.
   Sixth rainout of week: Saturday, 6:00 P.M.
   Seventh rainout of week: Saturday, 7:30 P.M.

   Rainouts not able to be played on Saturday should be scheduled on Sunday:

   First rainout of week: Sunday, 2:00 P.M.
   Second rainout of week: Sunday, 3:30 P.M.
   Third rainout of week: Sunday, 5:00 P.M.
   Fourth rainout of week: Sunday, 7:30 P.M.

4. Umpire crew of a rained-out game should handle the rain date. Home team manager is responsible for notifying umpires or scheduling other umpires if original crew cannot serve.

5. In Major- and Minor-League games, all substitutes must have entered the game by no later than the defensive half of the fourth inning.

6. Mercy Rule: If at the end of the fourth or fifth inning one team is leading by 10 or more runs, the umpire shall end the game.

7. Manager and Spectator Control: Team manager is responsible for keeping himself, his team, and his spectators under control. If abuse of umpires and/or team members occurs, umpire will ask manager to join him in warning the party that:

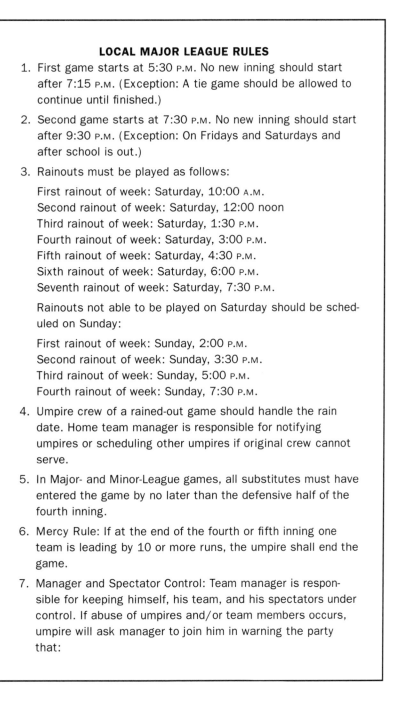

131

- He will be asked to leave the park if abuse continues.
- If he refuses to leave the park, the player he is supporting will be suspended and both will be asked to leave the park.
- In extreme cases, the game may be forfeited to the other team.

Managers and coaches must remain in the dugout at all times, except with the umpire's permission.

If a team manager or coach sets such a poor example that he is ejected from a game by an umpire, the incident should be reported by the umpire immediately after the game to the League president, who will determine if further disciplinary action is warranted.

Figure 8.3 *(continued)*

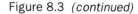

132

Mike Powers adds scorekeeping to the preseason training program in his league, requiring each team to assign an official scorekeeper and send that person to the scorekeeper's training meeting. Figures 8.4 and 8.5 are the materials that the St. Matthews Little League uses in its training.

Now, if you think you know Little League rules and would make a good umpire, take the Little League Baseball Quiz (Figure 8.6). The applicable rules appear in brackets after the questions, but if you still have doubts about the correct answer, check the answer key that follows.

SCOREKEEPING TRAINING

1. Home team keeps score; visitors announce the game.
2. Announcer controls the scoreboard.
3. Announcer:
   - If the teams have not taken their pregame warm-up, please announce: "Will the home team take the field for warm-up" or "Will the visiting team please take the field for warm-up." Each team is given 10 minutes for warm-up.
   - Announce the rosters with the player's jersey number and position.
   - Announce the first three batters at the beginning of each team's turn at bat.
   - Announce the players' names as they come into the batter's box and on deck: "The next batter is Joe Smith and Tom Doe on deck."
   - Announce the official starting time of the game after the first pitch.
   - After each half-inning, announce the team's hits, runs, and men left on base: "So-and-so team had 3 runs on 4 hits with 2 men left on base. The score is So-and-so team 5, Do-si-do team 3."
   - At the end of the game, announce that the home team is to bring in the flag and the bases (and in the Rookie League, the pitching machine).
4. Scorekeepers:
   - Please use the book marked August League.
   - Mark all plays and substitutions in the scorebook.
   - It is a good idea to bring an extra sheet of paper to jot down the substitutions and then record them in the scorebook.
   - Every player will have a slot in the scorebook for the August League scorebook. The August League uses the round-robin method of batting in both leagues.
   - Record at the bottom of the page the hits, runs, and errors.
   - If unsure on how to score a play, try to jot it down on the piece of paper longhand and then refer to notes later and score it in the book.
   - Use the position numbers for each player, not the abbreviation for the position: pitcher is 1, not P.

133

Figure 8.4 Scorekeeping training

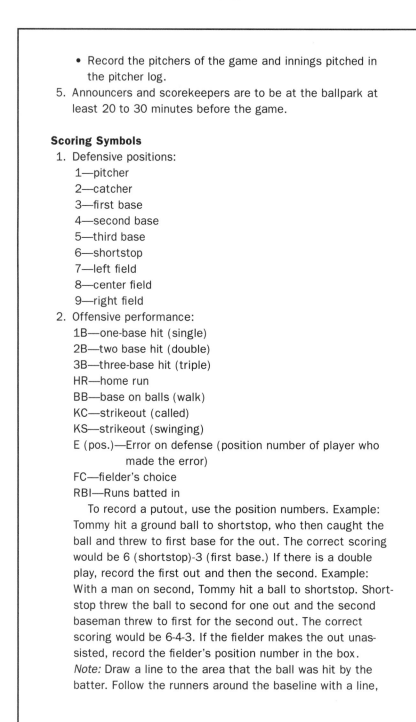

- Record the pitchers of the game and innings pitched in the pitcher log.
5. Announcers and scorekeepers are to be at the ballpark at least 20 to 30 minutes before the game.

Scoring Symbols
1. Defensive positions:
    1—pitcher
    2—catcher
    3—first base
    4—second base
    5—third base
    6—shortstop
    7—left field
    8—center field
    9—right field
2. Offensive performance:
    1B—one-base hit (single)
    2B—two base hit (double)
    3B—three-base hit (triple)
    HR—home run
    BB—base on balls (walk)
    KC—strikeout (called)
    KS—strikeout (swinging)
    E (pos.)—Error on defense (position number of player who made the error)
    FC—fielder's choice
    RBI—Runs batted in

   To record a putout, use the position numbers. Example: Tommy hit a ground ball to shortstop, who then caught the ball and threw to first base for the out. The correct scoring would be 6 (shortstop)-3 (first base.) If there is a double play, record the first out and then the second. Example: With a man on second, Tommy hit a ball to shortstop. Short-stop threw the ball to second for one out and the second baseman threw to first for the second out. The correct scoring would be 6-4-3. If the fielder makes the out unas-sisted, record the fielder's position number in the box. *Note:* Draw a line to the area that the ball was hit by the batter. Follow the runners around the baseline with a line,

Figure 8.4 *(continued)*

showing where they are at all times. You may lightly color in the diamond in the scorebook when a run scores.

3. Running symbols:
   SB—stolen base (catcher has the ball and runner advances)
   WP—pitcher throws a wild pitch past catcher and runner advances
   PB—catcher lets ball get passed him, runner advances
   B—balk
   E—error

Use these symbols to describe why the runners advanced.

Scoring Symbols Used in Score Book

1—Uniform number.

2—Name. There should be a slot for each player in the August League.

3—Position player is starting at. Not all players will have a starting position number.

4, 5—Inning and position substitution was made. Indicate if the substitution was made in the top of the inning or the bottom of the inning by placing a dot in the upper corner for the top of the inning or a dot in the bottom corner for the bottom of the inning.

6—Uniform number of player batting.

7—Number of outs.

8—Follow the players around the diamond. Show where the ball was hit. Lightly color in the diamond when a run scores.

9—Indicate what the batter does in this box.

10—Ball and strike counts. Follow the batter's count by checking off the appropriate box for each pitch.

11—RBIs. Place on top of the diamond and circle.

12—Runs, hits, and errors for each inning.

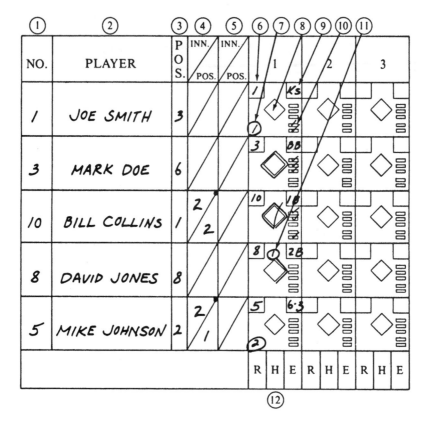

Figure 8.5 Sample score book page

LITTLE LEAGUE BASEBALL QUIZ: RULES

Name_____

Circle the correct answer: True or False.

1. Batter is out if he hits the ball with one foot outside
   the batter's box. [6.03 and 6.06 (a)]   T   F
2. Batter swings at third strike but is hit by the pitch,
   so goes to first. [6-08 (b)]   T   F
3. A batter can bunt on the third strike. [6.05 (d)]   T   F
4. A batter is out if he bunts down the first base line,
   running inside of it, and is hit by the thrown ball from
   the catcher to the first baseman. [7.09 (k)]   T   F
5. A substitute player must remain in the game until he
   has batted at least once and played at least six
   consecutive outs on defense. [3.03]   T   F
6. If two base runners end up on second base, . . .
   both runners are out. [7.03]   T   F
7. . . . second runner is automatically out. [7.031] T   F
8. . . . second runner has to be tagged out. [7.03]   T   F
9. A base runner is out if hit by a batted ball before a
   fielder touched it. [7.08 (f)]   T   F
10. A base runner is out if hit by a batted ball after it
    touches a fielder's glove. [7.09 (m)]   T   F
11. A team may not pitch three 12-year-old players in the
    same week. [Reg. VI (c)]   T   F
12. If a pitcher pitches four innings on Monday, he can
    still pitch two innings on Wednesday. [Reg. VI (b)] T   F
13. According to the infield-fly rule, the batter is
    automatically out if he hits an infield fly ball . . . with
    two outs and runners on first and second.   T   F
14. . . . with one out and runners on first and third.   T   F
15. . . . with no outs and the bases loaded.   T   F
16. . . . with one out and runners on first and second. T   F
17. If both managers agree the field is playable, the
    umpire must start the game. [3.10]   T   F
18. Batter receives a walk and catcher immediately asks
    for time-out, but batter rounds first and goes to
    second base. Umpire should make batter return to
    first. [5.10 (h)]   T   F

Figure 8.6 Little League baseball quiz

19. First baseman, in fair territory, reaches across the foul line to catch a foul fly, but the ball bounces off his glove into fair territory. It is a fair ball.　　T　F

20. Batted ball hits home plate and bounces in the air; catcher fields it in the air and throws runner out at first. Batter is out.　　T　F

21. A runner leaves second base too soon and scores on the batter's single, and umpire sees the play. The runner must return to third. [7.13]　　T　F

22. A runner may tag up and advance after a foul fly ball is caught. [7.08 (d)]　　T　F

23. Runner on first steals second on a foul tip caught by the catcher. Runner must return to first.　　T　F

24. Runner who runs more than three feet out of the base line to avoid interference with a fielder fielding a batted ball should be called out. [7.08 (q)]　　T　F

25. Runners on first and third, one out; batter is automatically out when he hits an infield fly.　　T　F

26. Catcher makes tag with back of gloved hand, which contains the ball, before the runner touches home plate. Runner is out.　　T　F

27. Runner on first is hit by a batted ball while standing on the base. Runner is out. [7.08 (f)]　　T　F

28. Runners on first and second, no outs. Batter hits infield fly, which hits runner while standing on first. Runner is out. [7.08 (f)]　　T　F

29. Batter bats out of turn and singles. With count 2 and 0 on next batter, appeal is made and first batter is called out. [6.07]　　T　F

30. Runner on third leaves base too soon on a fly ball and scores. Umpire sees the infraction and should call the runner out. [7.10 (q)]　　T　F

SCORE

ANSWER KEY

1. T	7. F	13. F	19. F	25. F
2. F	8. T	14. F	20. T	26. T
3. T	9. T	15. T	21. F	27. T
4. T	10. F	16. T	22. T	28. F
5. T	11. T	17. T	23. F	29. F
6. F	12. F	18. F	24. F	30. F

Figure 8.6 *(continued)*

9

STRATEGY FOR PLANNING A SUMMER INSTRUCTION LEAGUE

It seems that just as soon as the Little League season begins, it is coming to an end. Most leagues, especially those in the northern part of the country, are finishing toward the end of June. Of course, there are All-Star teams in the Major League division (11- and 12-year-olds) that are selected to play in the Little League All-Star tournament, culminating in the Little League World Series. They continue to play through July and August, depending on how far they advance. But these teams represent a very small percentage of players, probably no more than 10 percent—less than that in a very large program. Only those competing at the state championship level play through July. This is too early to stop playing ball with so much of the summer left. Just ask any Little Leaguers if they would like to continue playing. Their answer will show you why you should have a summer instructional league.

Little League Camp

Little League, Inc., sponsors a Little League Baseball Camp in Williamsport, Pennsylvania, and in several other regional facilities. Conducted in two-week sessions, it is very popular and fills up early. Call (570) 326-1921 for specific information and to make reservations. Teams are formed based on equivalent skill levels. The camp provides baseball instruction in the morning (see Figures 9.1, 9.2, and 9.3), and each team plays two games per day—one in the afternoon and another in the evening. Although there are some other activities, be assured that this is serious baseball for two weeks and about 20 games. Because the emphasis is on learning, some Little League rules are waived, such as not permitting coaches to go out on the field to instruct players during the games.

Setting Up Your Summer League

An instructional league can be operated by any Little League program locally. First, do your homework to make sure there are enough interested players to make it worthwhile to put it together. Next, contact your Little League district administrator to be sure your Little League insurance will cover the program. It should, but if for any reason it does not, find an insurance program that does. There should be at least two coaches/instructors for each team of 12 players. School coaches and/or college or high school baseball players are often available in the summer. If they do not have Little League experience, you will have to conduct a training school for them to make sure they are fully acquainted with Little League rules and objectives. Look for volunteers among your Little League organization, but some of the summer staff may have to be paid. In your Summer League budget, you should include caps and T-shirts as uniforms. A combination of funds from your Little League budget and the registration fees from parents should be enough to pay for your summer program. If not, you should consider planning a fund-raiser among the participants, and open the concession stand for the evening games.

Daily Schedule

This is a schedule we recommend:

9:00–Noon	Instruction and practice drills
Noon–1:00	Lunch
1:00–3:00	First game
3:00–4:00	Rest, skull session recap of game
4:00–5:30	Snack, pregame practice
5:30–7:00	Second game, with spectators

9.1 Players take turns learning second-base position during morning drill practice.

An alternative schedule is for the players to return home at four o'clock for rest and dinner and then return with their parents for the second game at six. It is recommended that the camp be for players who will be graduating from Tee Ball/Machine Pitch leagues this year and be eligible for Minor League next year, and for players through 11 years of age this year who will be eligible for Major League next year.

Summer Tournaments

Local tournaments on weekends during the summer will provide additional playing opportunities—and funds can be raised via the concession stand. Berlin Little League participates in three area tournaments each year, and hosts a fourth. There are generally two age brackets, coinciding with the Minor League (9 and 10) and Major League (11 and 12), with the possibility of scheduling both baseball and softball in both age groups, assuming your league has

9.2 Second baseman touches base on force play.

9.3 Getting rid of the ball quickly and accurately is drilled to infielders.

both. For your host tournament, entry fees of around $125 per team and concession stand revenue will help fund both your tournament and your summer instructional league. The two should not conflict, since the instructional league is during the week and the tournaments are on the weekends.

We recommend a double-elimination format, which guarantees that each team will play a minimum of two times. Brackets for planning such a tournament can be found on the Little League website: www.LittleLeague.org. To increase interest in your tournament, we also recommend staging skill competitions, such as home-run derbies and pitching speed booths. Naturally, awards should be given to the winning teams. Staging and participating in area tournaments is a great way to spend a summer weekend. If you can't stage a tournament alone, invite a neighboring Little League organization to sponsor it jointly.

There is just too much summer weather left to stop playing baseball in June!

Instructional League in St. Matthews

Mike Powers and his league in St. Matthews, Kentucky, had success with a summer instructional camp, held in conjunction with the University of Louisville. Instead of confining the camp to two weeks, they ran it for the month of August (after most All-Star teams are finished) and conducted it in the evenings as a summer league, with each team playing two games per week. They also had two leagues, one for 7- and 8-year-olds, and one for players 9, 10, and 11. Figure 9.1 is the information sheet for the St. Matthews Instructional League, and Figure 9.2 is the application form. The special game rules that were used in the St. Matthews Instructional League are shown in Figure 9.3.

Mike advocates a personal evaluation of each player at the end of the instructional league for both his use and the use of his coach next year. He uses an evaluation form to score the strengths and weaknesses of a player in the areas of hitting, pitching, and fielding. Mike's son Tom went to the Cardinal Baseball Camp, sponsored by the University of Louisville, and Mike uses evaluation forms similar to those developed by that camp. In Figures 9.4 and 9.5, Mike shares his son Tom's evaluation with us.

Each league has its own strengths and limitations for the conducting of a summer instructional league in terms of facilities and personnel. Be assured of one thing, however: You will have plenty of kids ready, willing, and eager to participate.

WHAT: St. Matthews August Instructional League
WHO: Any 7- to 11-year-old playing this year
TIME: Season opens July 28, and ends August 30
10-game schedule, 2 games per week—
weeknights only
COST: $15.00 per player
UNIFORMS: Cap and T-shirt included in cost
REASON: Improve fundamental skills, especially batting
LEAGUES: 7- to 8-year-olds: pitching machine pitch/no steals
or walks
9- to 11-year-olds: modified minor league rules

BRIEF SUMMARY OF MODIFIED INSTRUCTIONAL LEAGUE RULES

Both Leagues
1. Six innings or 1½ hours, whichever comes first
2. No pickup players allowed
3. Round-robin batting order
4. Minimum play: six outs on defense
5. Unlimited substitutions, except pitcher

9, 10, and 11 League
Regular Little League pitching rules, except: no player shall pitch more than 3 innings per game

If you have not been assigned to a team by July 16, or if you have any questions, ask or call:

Barbara Shaffer: (w) 555-1708; (h) 555-4212

Margaret Streck: (h) 555-8207

145

Figure 9.1 St. Matthews August Instructional League Information Sheet

PLEASE READ CAREFULLY

1. Fill in all information on this form. You will be called to supply missing data. Your application will not be processed until all information is available.

2. Enclose payment with application, place in envelope, seal, *print* name and age of child on envelope, and return to concession stand. Please pay by check—THERE WILL BE NO CASH RECEIPTS ISSUED. Sign-up deadline is *Saturday, June 21*.

PLEASE PRINT

Child's Name _____ Birth date _____

Parent's Name _____ Spouse _____

Address _____ Phone _____

Group Health Insurance Plan and Number _____

_____

1. Did you play in St. Matthews Little League this year? _____

   If so, what team? _____

2. If you played in another league: _____

   What league? _____

   Name/phone of coach _____

3. Do you anticipate any extended absence during the summer season (vacation, camp, etc.)? If so, when? _____

   _____

4. For car-pool purposes, *if possible*, place applicant on team with:

   _____

5. St. Matthews Little League runs on volunteer manpower. Will you help as ☐ Manager ☐ Coach ☐ Scorekeeper ☐ Other _____

_____
Signature of Parent or Guardian

Figure 9.2 St. Matthews August Instructional League Application

Little League Games

1. Use Little League Rules except as modified herein.
2. Unlimited substitution.
3. Bat the roster. (All substitutes bat in order prior to the leadoff batter hitting a second time, regardless of whether or not the substitute plays defensively.)
4. Pitcher is limited to a maximum three innings in any given game except once during the season when a team is scheduled to play on successive nights. Then, and only then, one pitcher may pitch six innings in one of the two games so scheduled.
5. No forfeits or rescheduling of rained-out games.
6. If one team has an insufficient number of players to field nine, said team may use a substitute from the opponent's roster.
7. Minor League 10-Run Rule (regular season) will apply—no team can score more than 10 runs in a half inning under any circumstances. When the 10th run is scored, the half inning is concluded regardless of number of outs, and the next half inning commences.
8. Length of the game is the same as the Minor League (regular season)—6 innings or 1½ hours of play, whichever comes first. This includes ties, since no won-lost records are kept.

Minor League Games

1. Use Little League Rules except as modified herein.
2. Unlimited substitution.
3. Bat the roster.
4. Pitches will be delivered to the batter by the pitching machine, operated and adjusted by the manager or coach of the offensive team.
5. There will be no walks or called strikes. However, once a batter has two strikes (swinging), the batter must swing at one of the next two pitches. If the batter hits a foul ball on said swing, the requirement of swinging at one of the next two pitches starts again. The penalty for failure to swing at one of the two pitches is a called strikeout.
6. Runners may not advance on catcher's return throws to the mound.

Figure 9.3 St. Matthews Instructional League special game rules

7. If a batted ball hits the pitching machine or the adult feeding the machine prior to touching a defensive player, the ball is declared dead, no advance by runners can occur, and the play is nullified. The batter returns to the plate and resumes his turn at bat.

8. If a ball thrown by the defense hits the pitching machine, it is a live ball and play continues.

9. No forfeits or rescheduling of rained-out games.

10. If one team has an insufficient number of players to field nine, said team may use a substitute from the opponent's roster.

11. Minor League 10-Run Rule (regular season) will apply—no team can score more than 10 runs in a half inning under any circumstances. When the 10th run is scored, the half inning is concluded regardless of outs, and the next half inning commences.

12. Length of the game is the same as the Minor League (regular season)—6 innings or 1½ hours of play, whichever comes first. No inning can begin after 1½ hours have elapsed. This includes ties, since no won-lost records are kept.

13. Adult coaches may be used.

14. The assigned umpire will be the umpire in charge and will exercise all decisions relative to rule interpretations. In addition, he will make all judgment calls on fly balls, call all bases except home plate, and keep account of the number of strikes on the batter. The assigned umpire will determine if the batter did swing and observe runners for leaving the base too soon.

15. In addition to the assigned umpire, one adult will be selected from the stands to assist. This assistance is limited to determining if a batted ball is fair (point) or foul (shout "Foul ball") and exercising judgment on safe/out calls at home plate only. It will not be necessary for this adult to wear the protective gear, since he will not be behind the catcher as the pitch is delivered.

Department of Athletics

University of Louisville
Louisville, Kentucky 40292
(502) 588-5732

UNIVERSITY of LOUISVILLE

PLAYER _Tom Powers_

CARDINAL BASEBALL CAMP
EVALUATION

HITTING

STRENGTHS	WEAKNESSES
____ Knuckles aligned *not aligned*	____ Hands apart
✓ Good starting position	____ Too low
✓ Top hand over	____ Hitches (props hands)
✓ Hands on bat to follow thru	____ Uppercut swing
✓ Good arm extension	____ No arm extension
✓ Smooth follow thru	____ Stops arms during swing
____ Good arm strength	____ Cannot handle bat
____ Bat in proper position	✓ Stiff front arm
✓ Eyes level to pitcher	____ Eyes slanted to pitcher
✓ Head stays on ball thru swing	____ Pulls head away from ball
____ Level shoulders	✓ Front shoulder too high
____ Front shoulder to ball	✓ Front shoulder pulls off ball
✓ Hips level thru swing	____ Hips locked
____ Hips open during swing	____ Hips do not point to ball
✓ Comfortable distance apart	____ Stance too narrow
✓ Good balance	____ Improper balance
____ Front foot open	✓ Closed front foot
✓ Good stride distance	____ Stride is too long
✓ Foot strides forward	____ Steps in bucket
	✓ Back foot moves

COMMENTS: _Radar gun speed 56_
Good tools. With good coaching could be an excellent
pitcher.

Academic and Athletic Excellence

149

Figure 9.4

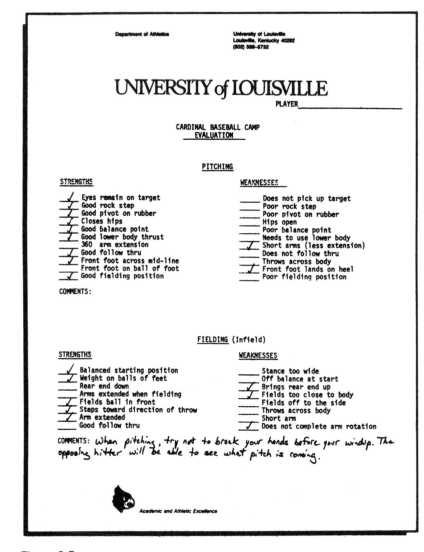

Figure 9.5

10

STRATEGY FOR WINNING

Is it incongruous, since we have been advocating "Keep it simple, make it fun," to have a final chapter on the subject of winning? Not at all. Given the choice of winning or losing, it's a cinch that your team will like winning a lot more—because it's more fun!

We both have outstanding records for managing winning teams during a combined 30 years of coaching following the philosophy of "Keep it simple, make it fun." Our definition of a winning team is simply a team that wins more games in a season than it loses. After all, winning can't be fully appreciated unless you can compare it to the humbling experience of losing. We can't guarantee you an undefeated season or a championship team, but we can virtually guarantee you a winning season—if you are willing to do what it takes to achieve it. It means following each of the elements of coaching that we have outlined in this book—plus one other: practice, practice, practice.

We mean practice *every* day. Baseball is a game of skills that can be perfected simply through repetitive drilling, practice after practice after practice. Take a young player who can't catch a fly ball and hit fly balls to that kid 200 times, and eventually the balls will be caught. Hit ground balls to a young infielder 200 times, and eventually they won't go through the legs anymore.

"But I can't take the time to practice my team every day," you say? We didn't say *you* have to be there every day, although it would be nice if you could. Your players will be there, you can bet on that. We encourage you to surround yourself with two or three coaches to help you. Surely you can arrange to have at least two of you there every day.

"But the parents will object," you say? "They will refuse to bring and pick up their child *every* day." Fast-forward ahead to the day that child makes the All-Star team, and the coach announces daily practice for the next three weeks so the team can prepare for the first All-Star tournament game. Will those parents refuse to bring and pick up their child every day for that? You know they won't. We think the child will persuade the parents that it is important to be at practice *every day*.

"But what if I can't get a practice field every day?" you say. Depending on field availability in your area, that could be a problem—one that requires a little ingenuity. A fence and a field can provide a place to practice batting (with the fence as the backstop) and catching fly balls. If your Little League complex has batting cages, one day's practice can be staged there; you can stagger the time each player is scheduled in the cage and have the on-deck batter hitting into a fence with a coach or player feeding the balls. Scheduling one skull session practice a week at your home will provide variety in your practice routine and will pay off in dividends: you will see your players put their heads into the game as well as their physical skills.

Let's review the things you need to do to have a winning season, in addition to practicing every day:

1. *Preseason planning strategy.* This includes the scouting that will help you draft good players who will make your team strong up the middle: pitchers, catcher, second baseman,

shortstop, center fielder. It includes recruiting good coaches—preferably three.

2. *Drills that make players good hitters.* Make it simple by teaching them the three-step "ready, aim, fire" elements of hitting. And teach them how to bunt so they can learn to track the ball.

3. *Drills that train four pitchers.* Concentrate on control, have them practice every day, and give them all some real pitching experience. Pick two who are in their last year of eligibility; then pick two who have two years left and can be groomed to be your top two pitchers next year. But above all else, teach pitchers how to control their fastball.

4. *Drills that build a strong defense.* In early practice, rotate your players at all positions until you can decide who are your best players for each position. Both on the field and in skull sessions, give infielders and outfielders situation drills, which will teach them how to react in actual games.

5. *Drills that make players aggressive base runners.* Teach players to "run when they walk" and turn at first base; teach them to slide; drill them in stealing second, third, and home; drill them in what to do when they are caught between bases; drill them in game situations, both on the field and in skull sessions. Drill your fast base runners in how to execute the "zebra" play. Since the runner will have to make a split-second decision, there should be a lot of drills in practice that simulate game situations.

6. *Drills that prepare players for game-winning situations, offensively and defensively.* Teach players how to analyze the opposing team's weaknesses and to take advantage of them—for example, accuracy of the catcher's throw to second; whether the pitcher backs up the catcher on a wild pitch with a runner on third; how far the third baseman plays off the

bag; how a new pitcher throws while he is warming up; substitutions in key "up-the-middle" positions, and so on.

7. *Breaking opponents' concentration.* Teach your players to exude confidence, to be vocal in encouraging their pitcher and their teammates, and to try to disrupt the concentration of opposing players. Base runners should fake leads to distract the baseman, pitcher, and catcher. Your catcher should carry on a running conversation with the pitcher, reminding the pitcher (and the batter) when there are two strikes—for example, "Way ahead of him," "Two strikes on him—he's gotta swing," and so on.

Charting

Charting is the paperwork of coaching that many coaches and managers just won't take the time to do. It is another test of how much time a manager and coaches are willing to devote to producing a winning team. We recommend keeping four charts: a time chart, a pitching chart, a fielding chart, and a batting chart.

The *time chart* is designed to record three significant running times for each player:

- The time to run from home to first
- The time to steal second
- The time to circle the bases

They are simple time tests, run periodically with a stopwatch, to keep a record of the relative speed of your players. In a crucial game where you would like a runner to steal second to get into scoring position, it helps to know how fast that player on first is.

The *pitching chart* is designed to record the following statistics each time a player pitches (whether in practice, a practice game, or a real game):

- Balls
- Low strikes
- High strikes
- Walks
- Strikeouts
- Hits
- Runs
- Batters hit
- Batters faced
- Total number of pitches (see Figure 10.1)

10.1 Keep track of how many pitches your pitchers throw. A young arm can tire easily.
Photo by Joey Gardner, the Daily Times, *Salisbury, Maryland*

The *fielding chart* is for keeping a running record on the defensive play of your team. It can be taken from the official scorebook after each game, provided you have taught your scorekeeper how to keep the score accurately. It should record for each player:

155

- Ground ball assists
- Infield putouts
- Pop-ups caught
- Fly balls caught
- Line drives caught
- Ground ball errors
- Pop-up errors
- Fly ball errors
- Thrown ball errors
- Attempted catching errors
- Passed balls (catcher)

The batting chart (Figure 10.2) is the typical batting average analysis used in major-league baseball. One important statistic is total times on base (TOB). It may be the most significant statistic of all in Little League, because a much higher percentage of runs is scored once a player gets on base (whether by walk, error, or hit) in Little League, compared to higher levels of baseball. Consequently, look carefully at a player's TOB percentage. If it is good, it shows that the player knows how to work a pitcher to get on base; the player is patient enough to work the pitcher for a walk and is savvy enough to know when to expect a "fat" pitch to hit. Usually a player with a good on-base average also strikes out rarely and is a good prospect for the leadoff batter. You will note that is true of the top two players in TOB in Figure 10.2: The two best TOB were also the two best in batting averages and both had few strikeouts. As a matter of fact, your lineup, after a few games, should be dictated by the performance of your players as measured by the batting chart.

Pitching Rotation

In our league, two games per week are scheduled for each team. This has created an ongoing debate among coaches on whether it is better to pitch your two best pitchers six innings each or have them go three and three in both games. It is a question that has no pat answer. Sometimes you start a pitcher with the intention of pitching him only three innings, but then he will have such an easy time in the first three innings, with good control and minimum pitches thrown, that it would be a mistake to change pitchers.

The biggest mistake Little League managers make with their pitching strategy is looking ahead to the next game instead of concentrating on winning the present game.

On the other hand, if you are charting your pitchers, you need to watch the number of pitches as an indication of how they are doing. If a pitcher gets behind on every batter, gives a lot of walks and hits, and your defense is committing a lot of errors, he may be throwing more pitches in three innings than he did in a previous

PLAYER	G	TAB	W	HP	S	OAB	H	TOB	R	2B	3B	HR	RBI	SO	BATT. AVG.
Lane Acree	7	14	0	0	0	14	6	6	4	0	2	0	2	5	.429
Jim Beirne	9	33	5	0	0	28	10	15	11	0	3	0	8	5	.357
Rod Blankenship	8	19	2	0	0	17	6	8	6	1	0	0	5	4	.353
Rodney Cox	9	13	3	1	0	9	2	6	0	0	0	0	0	6	.222
Jeff Girod	9	13	1	1	0	11	5	7	2	2	0	0	0	2	.455
Mike Grose	7	9	1	0	0	8	3	4	3	1	0	0	2	1	.375
John Hoard	9	20	4	0	0	16	6	10	3	1	0	0	0	3	.375
David Joo	9	25	4	0	0	21	11	15	8	0	2	0	7	4	.524
Mike Lipscomb	9	17	2	1	1	14	5	8	3	0	1	0	3	8	.357
Jim McIntosh	9	34	6	0	1	27	15	21	12	1	0	0	6	4	.556
Mark Proctor	9	35	5	0	1	29	17	22	13	2	0	1	9	0	.586
Chuck Thomas	9	16	1	0	0	15	7	8	3	0	0	0	6	2	.467
Mike Walton	9	17	3	1	0	13	2	5	3	0	0	0	0	10	.154
Paul Williams	9	30	5	0	0	25	12	17	9	5	2	1	13	6	.480

KEY: G (games); TAB (total times at bat); W (walk); HP (hit by pitched ball); S (sacrifice); OAB (official times at bat); H (hits); TOB (total times on base); R (runs scored); 2B (doubles); 3B (triples); HR (home runs); RBI (runs batted in); SO (strikeouts); Batt. Avg. (batting average—number of hits divided by official times at bat).

10.2 Team averages, first half (9 games)

six-inning game. You often hear TV and radio play-by-play announcers comment on how many pitches a pitcher has thrown. Why do you think they consider it a significant statistic? When was the last time you kept track of that statistic on your pitchers?

Another mistake many Little League managers make is keeping pitchers in the game too long when they aren't being effective. This is another case where your statistics can help you—ask the coach who is doing the chart how many pitches the pitcher has thrown, how many low strikes, and how many walks.

Yanking a pitcher can be more traumatic to a child (and his parents) in Little League than in higher levels of baseball, but there is a gentle way to do it. Warn your pitcher first that you may have to replace him, and when you do, have the pitcher take another position rather than taking a downhearted walk to the dugout. Ironically, your pitcher rarely disagrees with you about the change; he is the one most acutely aware that he doesn't have it, and you can help his morale by reminding him that all pitchers are like that: "Some days they have it, and other days they don't."

The decision about taking a pitcher out is dictated in part by who you have left to put in. As mentioned in the chapter on pitching, you need four players capable of pitching. Any fewer, and you may find yourself in a difficult situation. Any more will mean that you will not be giving some of them enough work to keep in good pitching shape.

In terms of pitching strategy, we mentioned in the pitching chapter that your pitcher should concentrate on throwing low strikes to the top four or five batters in the opposing lineup, with an occasional change-up or curveball when ahead on the count. The four or five players in the lower end of the lineup, should just be challenged with fastballs. The pitcher can even pitch to them from the stretch position, which will reduce speed but improve control. The last thing you want is a walk to a weak hitter.

A pitcher's concentration may be so intense (as it should be) that he will forget his fielding responsibility when the time comes. That is where you must do your part as a coach. For example, with a runner on third remind your pitcher to cover home if the ball gets through the catcher; in a bunting situation, remind your pitcher (as well as the other infielders) to watch for a bunt. Study the other manager's signals and try to pick up the bunt sign. It is always amusing when you can do that and call out to your infield, "Watch for the bunt," just after the manager has flashed the bunt sign to his batter. The look on the batter's face of "Now what do I do?" is always priceless!

A great morale booster for a pitcher after a strikeout (when the bases are empty) is to have the catcher fire the ball to the third baseman, and as the infield folds in toward the pitcher's mound, the ball is tossed from third baseman to second baseman to shortstop, back to the third baseman, who hands the ball to the pitcher. Teammates, at the mound, give the pitcher encouragement and it not only boosts his confidence but puts a little extra apprehension in the mind of the next batter, witnessing that burst of enthusiasm. This exercise is diagrammed in Figure 10.4 and should be drilled in practice.

10.3 A conference between the manager, his pitcher, and the catcher helps to develop strategy.

Batting Strategy

The first four positions in your batting order should be filled with your best hitters, for the obvious reason that they will get more times at bat. Your leadoff batter should be a player who has a high

159

TOB percentage. As mentioned earlier, that player will rarely strike out, which means that he will either walk or make contact with the ball, which will get him on base via either a hit or an error.

The second batter in the lineup may be your best bunter, and should also have a high TOB percentage. The third batter in the

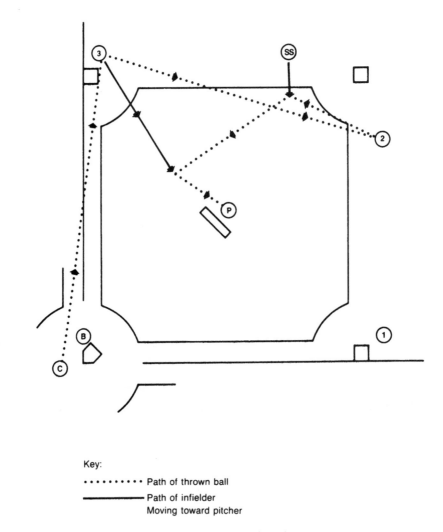

160

Key:

· · · · · · · · · Path of thrown ball

———————— Path of infielder
Moving toward pitcher

10.4 After-strikeout drill (with no one on base)

lineup should be your best hitter, and your fourth-place batter your best slugger. (Sometimes your best hitter in batting average will be a singles hitter, whereas your best slugger will be an extra base hitter—when he connects.) Rarely substitute in the first four or five places in the lineup, knowing that the combination of your best hitters, back-to-back, will come up to bat at least three times during the game.

Consider it a bonus when one of the batters in the lower half of the lineup gets on base, and plan the strategy of coaxing a walk with them more so than with the good hitters on the team. Give the take sign more often on a 2-0, or 3-1 count and *always* give it on a 3-0 count, to a player in the lower half of the batting order. Statistically we have found that two out of every three walks result in a run, so play for the averages and try to get your weak hitters on base any way you can.

Don't use the major-league strategy of having a batter bunt on the first pitch if there is a runner on first with fewer than two outs. Because there are so many wild pitches and passed balls in Little League, it is the exception when a runner on first doesn't get an easy steal to second. However, to help create a wild pitch or passed ball, give the fake-bunt sign, telling the batter to lean over the plate and pull back only at the last moment, in order to distract both pitcher and catcher. That will often get your runner to second base without sacrificing the batter. Even if it doesn't work, it will have the infield coming in on the next pitch, expecting a bunt, while you have given the hit sign. If the batter makes contact with the ball, it will probably go through for a hit.

Baserunning Strategy

We mentioned the strategy of "run when you walk" in the chapter on baserunning, but sometimes your batters have to be reminded when the time comes. A code word like "Tiger!" will remind them without tipping off the opposition. We have seen the strategy of taking an extra base work with some teams nearly every time, particularly if they are not strong up the middle defensively and are caught off guard by the play.

Constant reminders from the dugout to your base runners and base coaches are necessary. Before every pitch is not too often to point out the situation:

- "No outs—don't take chances."
- "Two outs—run on anything."
- "You're forced on a ground ball" (see Figure 10.5).
- "Tag up on a fly."

One of the most critical base-running plays, and one that requires coaching, comes up when a runner is on third. If a wild pitch or passed ball occurs, the runner has to decide whether to attempt to steal home. As coach, you must have done your part in analyzing the following:

- Does the pitcher cover home?
- Does the catcher toss his helmet or try to see the play through the face guard?
- Is the catcher a rookie or experienced?
- Is the pitcher a rookie or experienced?
- Is the runner on third fast?

You have to evaluate the situation and then let your runner know what to do ahead of time. Trying to coach the runner *when* the situation occurs is almost impossible, since she will be hearing all kinds of advice from parents and teammates at the same time.

We will try our situation play called "zebra" with a runner on third base if some of these conditions are present:

- Our base runner is fast.
- There are two outs and a weak hitter is at bat.
- The third baseman and/or catcher are rookies.

The idea of the play is for the base runner to deliberately draw a throw from the pitcher or catcher and force a rundown between third and home. The situation in which it is most likely to succeed is when the third baseman plays off the bag, which gives the runner the chance to go three or four steps down the line after each pitch (see Figure 10.6). The runner should make a break for the plate the instant the catcher throws the ball to either the pitcher or the third baseman, because while the runner is running and sliding into home, the ball has to be thrown and caught twice, from the catcher and then back to the catcher. That means five chances of an error: two throwing, two catching, and one tagging. If you have a fast runner with a three- or four-step lead, your chances are good!

10.5 You have to remind runners to run on a ground ball to avoid the force-out.

163

Motivational Strategy

Managing kids can be so frustrating sometimes, but so rewarding most of the time. At the Little League age, they are so trusting and so impressionable that it places a heavy responsibility on the adult who is their leader to justify their trust and impress them in a positive way.

Keeping things in perspective is the coach's biggest challenge. The pressure to win makes it very difficult for a coach to empathize

10.6 When the third baseman plays way off the bag, the base runner can move far down the line after the pitch crosses the plate—an ideal situation for the "zebra" play.

with the player who just blew it and lost the game. But empathize he must! A pat on the back or a reassuring word, instead of a dirty look or a chewing out, can go a long way toward defusing the pressure and sense of failure the "goat" is feeling.

Getting the coach's approval is important to a kid, and the sensitive coach will soon recognize how great a motivator encouragement is. However, a coach also has to recognize that levels of accomplishment vary greatly among the players on the team. What is a routine play for an All-Star is a milestone for a rookie.

In *Managing Little League Baseball*, there is a discussion of "Stargell Stars" and what great motivators they are. Hall of Famer Willie Stargell, when he was team captain of the world-champion Pittsburgh Pirates, gave gold-plated stars to his teammates when they made exceptional plays, and they pinned them on their caps. We bought some inexpensive felt stars, and we award them to players after each game, based on exceptional performance at each child's level of ability. All rookies get a star when they get their first hit and their first putout in the field. One kid who was still looking for his first star at midseason was the only player to help the coaches clean out the dugout after a game, and he earned a star for that.

The point is that any player who does something special *for him or her* to help the team gets a star. The kids line up after each game—win or lose—as if we are giving out gold pieces instead of felt stars.

In a way, the "Stargell Star," which recognizes a player's contribution to the team, is the exact opposite of the winning-is-everything philosophy in sports that unfortunately creeps into Little League baseball sometimes.

As a manager or coach, you will have a winning season if you put in the necessary time and your players practice, practice, practice. And you personally will be a winner in the eyes of your kids if they remember you as a coach who always recognized their triumphs and empathized with their defeats. Long after they have forgotten the scores of the games, they will still remember the coach who cared about them.

Index

***Boldfaced** *page numbers indicate illustrations.*